analyzing and predicting
JUVENILE DELINQUENCY
with the MMPI

EDITED BY

STARKE R. HATHAWAY, DIRECTOR, DIVISION OF CLINICAL
PSYCHOLOGY, DEPARTMENT OF PSYCHIATRY AND NEUROLOGY
UNIVERSITY OF MINNESOTA

ELIO D. MONACHESI, CHAIRMAN, DEPARTMENT OF SOCIOLOGY
UNIVERSITY OF MINNESOTA

THE UNIVERSITY OF MINNESOTA PRESS, Minneapolis

PRINTED AT THE COLWELL PRESS, INC., MINNEAPOLIS

Library of Congress Catalog Card Number: 53-8615

HV
9069
.H34

PUBLISHED IN GREAT BRITAIN, INDIA, AND PAKISTAN BY

GEOFFREY CUMBERLEGE: OXFORD UNIVERSITY PRESS, LONDON, BOMBAY, AND KARACHI

Analyzing and Predicting
Juvenile Delinquency with the MMPI

Acknowledgments

M ANY individuals and groups have, in one way or another, contributed to the work described in this volume and it is a pleasure to acknowledge their contributions.

To the Graduate School of the University of Minnesota we owe special thanks since the funds it so generously provided over the years made our work possible. The Frederick B. Wells research grant to the Department of Psychiatry and Neurology, University of Minnesota Medical School, also aided us greatly.

We are indebted to the personnel of the Minneapolis public school system for granting us permission to administer the MMPI to their ninth-grade pupils during the academic year 1947–48. We are especially grateful to the principals, counselors, and teachers of the Minneapolis public schools for the aid they gave us in the collection of data. We also owe thanks to the administrative and teaching personnel of the University of Minnesota High School for similar aid. For the data obtained from the St. Cloud, Minnesota, ninth-graders on November 15, 1948, we wish to thank H. B. Gough, superintendent, and J. M. Lunemann, principal.

We wish to thank James H. Ashbaugh, Dorothy Bell, Dora F. Capwell, W. Grant Dahlstrom, Dr. Donald W. Hastings, and Margaret Lauber for their willingness to have their work included in this volume.

Efficient research assistance was contributed by the following: Dorothy Bell, Carl H. Cornell, Leona Erickson Dahlstrom, Kathleen M. Darley, Mary Lee Erickson, Lorraine Kessler James, Elizabeth Leonard, Elsie Nordstrom, Beverly Peterson, Irving Simos, Marietta B. Spencer, May Lyon Sutton, and Ruth Thomas.

For clerical and stenographic aid, thanks are due to Helen Bambenek, Pat Benn, Helenann Clarke, Rhoda Hirsh, Carol J. Howe, Donald Jobes, Shirley Knudsen, Mary M. Nelson, Shirley Peterson, Lorraine Schmitzer, Nola Sarkis, Donna Sweet, and Gordon Wick.

In the study reported by one of the editors (Monachesi), the following former graduate students in the University of Minnesota assisted in the collection and analysis of the data: Eleanor M. Barnett, Paul M. Berry, Edith A. Bohince, Viola M. Brandon, Robert Dacy, Katherine Eustis, Dorothy D. Hayes, Gordon Jaeck, Ruth E. L. Johnson, Edward J. Kosciolek, Mercida M. Krips, Mary D. Meko, Vincent P. Reis, Grace L. Solether, Olaf H. Swenson, and Matilda Wallblom.

Thanks are also due to the officials of the Minneapolis Crime Prevention Bureau, the Hennepin County, Minnesota, Probation Office and the Ramsey County, Minnesota, Probation Office, for permission to examine their records.

We gratefully acknowledge the permission granted us by the editors of the *Journal of Applied Psychology* and the *Journal of Criminal Law, Criminology and Police Science* to use materials already published in these journals.

For excellent editorial work on the manuscript we are indebted to Jeanne Sinnen of the University of Minnesota Press.

STARKE R. HATHAWAY

ELIO D. MONACHESI

Table of Contents

Analyzing and Predicting
Juvenile Delinquency with the MMPI

Juvenile Delinquency and the MMPI

THE NEED is great for much more knowledge of the patterns of personality that lead to criminal and other maladjustive behavior. For example, many aspects of the mental hygiene movement rest upon the assumption that therapeutic work with individual children will decrease the likelihood of their later delinquency or mental illness. Actually there is little acceptable experimental evidence to support this assumption. But even if we did know that special therapeutic efforts would decrease the later incidence of maladjustment, we have no established, practical, reliable, and valid survey method for identifying the various subgroups of children that are more likely than others to have trouble. We must either blindly do general preventive work on whole populations or wait for children to become deviant in behavior and then offer treatment, depending upon the unhappy fact that a person already in trouble is more likely than others to have additional trouble.

These facts about the therapeutic situation are not changed by choosing to work with children classified into subgroups according to some common stress variable such as living in a slum area or in a broken home. Such factors are not indigenous characteristics of the individual children. Many children in a slum area do not become delinquent although the rate for delinquency among them is high. It can be assumed that those who do become so are susceptible because they have any one of several types of personality that makes them vulnerable to the slum-area stress. Those who do not become delinquent have other types of personalities that do not leave them vulnerable. In other words, clearing the slums will lower the delinquency rate, but this slum clearance is not individual therapy. We could have the same good effect upon the delinquency rate by taking susceptible children out of those slums and replacing them with resistant ones. But if we chose to adopt such a procedure (which of course we would

3

not) how would we discover these susceptible children? For that we should need understanding and analysis of the personality patterns of delinquents—whether they live in slums or in high-rent areas.

The great bulk of published studies undertaken to discover the personality characteristics of young people who later develop behavioral disorders have been based upon data collected after the individual became deviant. Usually the established fact of maladjustment has brought the individual to the attention of some agency, which then initiates a systematic attempt to relate his background to his present status. A considerable portion of our meager knowledge regarding the premonitory symptoms of maladjustment, therefore, is derived from a reconstruction of the deviant individual's developmental past.

Although this kind of reconstruction has provided valuable data on premonitory symptoms of coming personality disorders, the method involves many hazards. The reliability of the data is dependent upon the cooperativeness and credibility of informants as well as upon the accuracy of official public records. But even if absolute reliance could be placed upon the information contained in the case records, such information is hard to organize into objective and standardized categories; it is even more difficult and impractical to reduce case history material to well-defined and manipulable variables.

The difficulties inherent in methods that use data based upon social records or memory and summarization of past experiences are particularly important when one attempts to review the past personality of an individual deviant. Having become delinquent, he is a product of conscious and unconscious trends that he cannot be trusted to recall; nor can we safely infer such historical motivations with greater certainty. Control group methods, using the case history approach, are also suspect since the collection of information is inevitably colored by the knowledge on the part of informants and investigator that the present status of the experimental or control case needs or does not need explanatory findings. This largely nullifies the value of the controls. It is often disregarded that even the most objective among us is likely to recall freely the colorful adverse incidents in a boy's life if associations in the recall are prompted by the knowledge that the boy has persistently stolen automobiles. Public records may perhaps not be distorted by the investigators, but these records themselves have already been distorted in the routine processes of their compilation, and public records rarely provide comparable data on the individuals of the control group. It is probably a cultural characteristic that we seek to rationalize aberrant behavior and further the rationalization by unconsciously biasing information that requires subjective evaluation or recall.

What we seem to need ideally is the collection of data directly from the behavior of the subject himself before the occurrence of the maladjustment, data which are not at that time subject to interpretation or selection by the subject or others in terms of the outcome variable. But such a procedure, involving as it does longitudinal collection of data and longitudinal variation of the possible influencing factors in the environment, requires very large-scale surveys, and these, in turn, require simplicity and objectivity in the data collection methods that are used. These requirements are particularly troublesome when among all the persons included in the survey, only a small percentage will later fall into the experimental group.

When we attempt to make some practical use of data now widely considered related to asocial behavior—as, for example, in selecting groups of delinquency-prone children for especially appropriate group therapy—we encounter the problem of applying simple scaled variables to every subject. Although certain social factors such as broken homes or lack of community play areas are, or are now thought to be, conducive to delinquency or mental breakdown, the large-scale collection of the pertinent data for the variables is not a feasible project even in the comparatively simple pattern of a school system. It is most desirable, therefore, that we develop instruments permitting simple routine testing, yielding objective scores, and having sufficient reliability and validity so that wide-scale, low-cost estimates of the likelihood and type of trouble for each child would be practical.

The pioneer work of Capwell (4, 5, also Study 1), and the later checks of her findings as published by Monachesi (42, 43, 44, also Study 2), strongly suggested that the Minnesota Multiphasic Personality Inventory (36) might be such an instrument. (Hereafter the instrument is referred to simply as the MMPI.)

The MMPI is perhaps, in certain respects, not an ideal instrument for use at junior and senior high school levels. On the other hand, it is well suited to large-scale administration and objective scoring. Its scales include not only the usual neurotic and psychotic factors as observed in adult maladjustment but also indicators of the psychopathic deviate and paranoid behavior disorders. It is about as complex in variety of scales as can be handled with present statistical approaches and reasonable numbers of cases. On the other hand, it does not have so few variables that it greatly restricts the variety of personality patterns that could appear. Also, MMPI items are of considerable variety and there are 550 of them, so that the answers provide a good source for item study and the possible development of new analytic scales more particularly adapted to teen-age levels.

In addition, the MMPI is very widely used and many clinicians have a considerable body of objective and subjective information about the meaning of profiles which, while not always safely transferable to results obtained on younger people, is nevertheless an invaluable source of indications to be checked by one means or another. There is also extensive literature on the instrument, which again provides very frequent suggestions for interpretation or further research.

The purpose of this book is to collect in one volume the more representative of the presently available results of MMPI studies in juvenile delinquency. The findings of the various papers are chiefly developed toward the practical use of MMPI profiles for the understanding and prediction of unsocial behavior. We have deliberately given little space to development of the theoretical implications of the findings. Strong evidence is presented that MMPI variables can be rather closely predictive of good or bad social adjustment. We are not at this time chiefly concerned with why this should be so although such lines of thought provide tempting possibilities for later development.

We do not wish to give the impression that the MMPI is the only instrument that might have been used with comparable results, or that it is an ideal one to be adopted for all future work. The reasons for its choice rest upon the advantage given by the accumulated experience with it, the objective validity of the instrument, and, in comparison with some other personality tests, the greater variety of profiles that can result from it. We do feel very strongly that personality is so exceedingly complex and the number of different patterns of personality leading to delinquency or other maladjustment in an individual is so great that it is unjustifiable to work with only a few personality variables or scales.

THE MEANING OF DELINQUENCY

The term *juvenile delinquent* does not have constant meaning. It can be restricted to those juveniles who repeatedly commit crimes for which they are tried and sentenced, or it can be broadened to include any juvenile who is a nuisance to some of the adults with whom he comes into contact. Used in too severe a meaning the term will not include enough cases for any kind of meaningful study, both because few juveniles are that bad and because many with fairly bad personality traits and behavior do not happen to be repeatedly processed by the courts and found guilty. Used in too lenient a sense the term loses significance by coming to designate a host of mildly misbehaving juveniles who are really acceptably normal in personality but merely unfortunate enough to come under the scrutiny of adults or agencies with minimal tolerance for deviations from their own principles of social behavior.

In our discussions here we shall not attempt to be entirely consistent but we shall use the term *juvenile delinquent* to mean that at the least the individual has presumptively been guilty of offenses considered severe enough by law enforcement agencies to justify placing his name on the public records. The name's occurrence in the record is prima-facie evidence. We shall also include youngsters whose names do not appear in the records but who are known to have committed acts comparable to the acts of those whose names did get in.

We shall assume that delinquency is a symptom rather than a personality trait. This means that we expect to find a number of personality types among whom the symptom delinquency is common. We believe there is some value in differentiating the symptomatic behavior into classes (type of offense, grades of severity, and the like) but we have not been impressed from the available findings that this is a very fruitful approach. We choose to direct our attention chiefly to the differentiation of the personality types that frequently develop delinquency and, equally, of those types that infrequently become delinquent.

The problem of analyzing and predicting delinquency is not merely one of testing for abnormal characteristics for which delinquent behavior is a frequent symptom. To some extent personality characteristics that predispose the individual to delinquency are normal in young people. An excess of these general characteristics in a certain youth could require unusual control to prevent the occurrence of antisocial acts, and we could safely predict that persons with the greatest amount of energy (or whatever other factor is in excess) would be most likely to show undesirable behavior. However, among such cases, the most significant quality one might expect to measure would be the youth's acceptance of the controls of society so that his exuberant impulses are suppressed or acceptably modified. It is probable that many nondelinquent youths are so, not because they lack the personality pattern of delinquency insofar as that relates to impulses toward reprehensible acts, but rather because, even with this excess of normal youthful impulse, they likewise have greater control or have learned the controls suggested by the culture. Incidentally, one may think of such controls as occasionally exceeding normal needs and in such a case a youth could be overcontrolled, leading (in accord with some lines of current psychopathological theory) to the development in him of a neurotic syndrome.

MENTAL ILLNESS VERSUS DELINQUENCY

There is much theory, but little definitive evidence, relating the adjustment patterns as they are seen in adult mental illness to the diverse acts contributing to delinquency in late adolescence. One may find every degree of expressed or implicit faith, from the assumption that delinquency is symptomatic of mental illness similar to adult patterns, to the opposite assumption that delinquency is a personality pattern almost wholly related to distorted or uninhibited normal personality and occurring in a person having freedom of choice as to whether he shall or shall not commit an act.

Under the first line of thinking, delinquency would be identified with our attitudes toward mental illness and punishment would never be indicated, except as it might be related to a retraining therapeutic procedure. The delinquent would, like the insane, be free of censure because he is not considered responsible for his acts. At the other extreme, since the person is assumed to be operating under more normal impulses which are poorly controlled, punishment and training and exhortation are the indicated methods of approach; the delinquent and those responsible for him are censured morally.

If a delinquent adolescent does things that are asocial or violent, involving the cultural concept of breaking the law, he is usually handled by the institutions and persons concerned with the enforcement of laws and protection of society. He is apprehended and examined by the police and is duly processed in court or by other agencies that will consider the possibility of confinement or other restraint to control him in his dereliction of will. By contrast, if the aberrant behavior of the maladjusted child is not destructive or violent against persons, the tendency is to send him to a professional clinic for assessment as a psychologically ill person.

This contrast in handling has led to an unresolved conflict in which part of the misbehaving adolescents are referred to psychiatric or psychological clinics and part are allowed to be processed in the usual pattern as dictated by the law. To a major extent these contrasting decisions are automatically dictated by the nature of the aberrant acts, but often the acts are hard to classify or the child happens to have someone in his environment who will intercede and demand special treatment. Sometimes this special treatment is in the direction of careful psychological study and sometimes it takes the form of especially severe punishment. Often two persons who have committed identical acts are routed into these two divergent paths. In other cases the courts themselves transfer some of the responsibility to the clinic or hire a clinical staff, and the action patterns are mixed.

There is very little scientific evidence or even theoretical backing for a preference among these practices, however varied they are. It is to be hoped that the findings in the studies reported here will provide more facts on which our attitudes and actions regarding the delinquent can be based.

The scales of the MMPI derive from psychiatric practice. Every scale and combination of scales shows a moderate relationship to patterns of adult maladjustment. If delinquency is symptomatic of neurotic or psychotic personality syndromes, then one would expect groups of juvenile delinquents to show significant elevations on scales of the MMPI. If, on the other hand, delinquency results from patterns of personality not represented in psychiatric practice, then MMPI scales will not show significant relationships to the occurrence of delinquency. We feel that, as long as we lack better approaches, delinquents showing MMPI profiles with patterns analogous to the ones from mentally ill persons (or similar findings on other tests with established validity or other acceptable evidence) should, for the sake of consistency if for no other reason, be handled with emphasis upon the clinical approach. (We deliberately avoid the word *treatment* because in the sense of specific prescriptions for symptoms it has little established validity. But professional clinicians are used to the course and probable development of the familiar mental disorders and make appropriate decisions on the basis of that knowledge.) Of course clinical evaluation and recommendations must conform to the needs of society. For society's protection, incarceration or close supervision may be needed; but these should be used more like prescriptions in individual cases, not as stereotyped applications of law.

If we find that other delinquents do not show personality patterns that are analogous to recognized mental illness, then these need further study. Some would argue that we should simply enlarge the concept of mental illness to include all delinquents. This would suggest the idealistic but impractical attempt to study and treat all delinquents as mental patients. We at present reject this in favor of the better among modern practices which have at least historical evolution to recom-

mend them. Meanwhile we would continue our studies in psycho-
pathology; perhaps by such study we can isolate from among these
unclassified delinquents type after type, each meriting a categorical
designation according to causation, treatment, or course of disorder,
until there is a negligible undifferentiated remainder.

In brief, we take the preliminary stand that delinquency, as seen
from individual case to individual case, manifests multiple personality
patterns. Among such patterns may be the neurotic, psychotic, character disorder, and other syndromes that appear in adult mental illness.
As such recognized personality deviations are isolated among the
juvenile offenders, the remainder of less easily classifiable delinquent
cases may be studied for analysis and understanding with some confidence that the problems have been simplified by the reduction in
types of cases.

ANALYSIS VERSUS PREDICTION

The two tasks of analyzing the various types of personality problems that often lead to delinquency and of predicting the delinquency
by a probability number are closely related but not identical en-
deavors. Our present chief intent is the former, but we are aware that
the reader is likely to be more concerned with routine prediction. It is
not possible to be very efficient in preventive activities with nondelinquent groups when one is forced to use a blunderbuss approach
knowing that a good deal of effort is expended on children not much
in need of it. Likewise we cannot be efficient or inspired in work which
is not determined in its aims by some knowledge of the personality
characteristics most clearly contributing to the delinquent behavior
we hope to prevent. For prediction with an objective test a mere
"delinquency scale" might do, but for differential analysis among delinquents we need to use independently established scales that have
at least a presumptive relationship to causes or other data apart from
the delinquency itself. If analytic scales are properly valid and applied to greatest advantage then perhaps they will yield prediction
statistics more useful than those from a special delinquency-proneness
scale; a special scale can never do the analysis job and so is always
seriously limited in what it can contribute.

As the papers collected here show, the regular MMPI profiles are
useful for predictive statements and in general for preliminary differentiation of delinquents from nondelinquents. By item analysis or the
use of regression weights or other statistics, prediction numbers as
shown in these papers could be made better. But while we want to

provide estimates of the probability of delinquency, we want also to maintain what meaning there is in the MMPI profiles. Prediction scales have only predictive import. They continue to use the old approach that considers delinquency as though it were a unitary personality entity. This simplified approach encourages the sterile attitude that those who become delinquent are so alike that we can talk about them and treat them in a single category—The Juvenile Delinquent.

We hope in future publications to separate more completely the analysis of the delinquent personality from the prediction of delinquency by a more refined treatment of the data if this is necessary, in order to develop more fully the predictive potentialities. In the present series the data are adapted toward the relationship of delinquency to the familiar clinical disorders; and references and tables on the prediction of delinquency are given as important preliminary data from the scales as they are now used. Of course we are aware that if more fundamental syndromes and variables could be discovered, then the problems of analysis and prediction would merge into one.

THE LIMITATIONS ON PREDICTION

At the outset in attempting prediction, we can hardly expect any instrument to appear perfectly accurate when the prediction is based upon data obtained before delinquency develops. Many individuals who show personality traits likely to give rise to delinquency (and thus who would have a relatively high probability of becoming delinquent) never happen into a stimulus situation that would encourage their actual delinquency. Other persons who have moderately delinquency-prone personalities (and who would, therefore, not have a high probability of becoming delinquent) find themselves in such facilitating environmental situations that delinquent acts do occur. Both of these environmental situations operate to reduce the validity of committed and recognized delinquency as a standard against which we can evaluate measured personality traits as predictive variables. Since it is not possible to predict with certainty the particular environmental circumstances that will operate on a given youth to inhibit or develop delinquency, the best we can expect is the identification in him of personality patterns that have a usefully high probability relation to later recognized delinquency.

It is interesting to realize that if we use a preventive program on an unselected population and if 20 per cent is the regular delinquency rate, then our program must handle 80 persons out of each 100 who

would not be delinquent anyway in order to work with the 20 who
would be. When we refer to increased efficiency in programs dealing
with delinquency we assume situations that involve this problem.
One could afford much better programs *per individual* if the group to
be treated was made up of children with higher relative probabilities of
delinquency.

We feel that, in actual figures, the top experimental prediction value
(correct percentage of expected delinquency) we can hope for among
a selected group cannot be greater than 90 and may be as low as 60 per
cent of accuracy. This is a discouragingly large range and the margin
to be gained by measurement as contrasted to less scientific procedures
could be small. Yet, considering our limited clinic and social agency
facilities and the high cost of each criminal to society and the individual, any improvement at all in the accuracy of prediction (and
thus, we hope, improvement in efficiency of preventive measures) is
worth much effort. We only wish to remind the reader of the rigorous
task we face and that we should not expect perfect validity in our
measurement devices before we put them to work.

As is implied in the discussion above we believe that the best prediction figures for actual delinquency would require the combination
of two measures obtained from two approaches. The first of these is
the measurement of the pertinent personality variables in the individual, and the second is the evaluation of the environmental factors
that provide opportunity and stimulus for delinquent acts and that
establish the definition of what behavior will be called delinquent.
In practice, all measures, whether purporting to be chiefly of personality or of environment, are in some degree mixtures of the two. It is
our feeling that of these, the personality variables are more closely
and usefully related to delinquency than are the environmental variables acting on the individual. We also feel that among modern personality evaluation methods there is much more likelihood of finding
practicable delinquency indicators by using objective personality tests
than by any other approach.

The validity of these initial hypotheses will be in part tested by the
data from the studies in this volume. The Capwell study on delinquent
and nondelinquent girls was the first to be published having such data
in statistical form. (The form of the MMPI used in her study, and
which therefore was of necessity used in the follow-up study that con-
stitutes the fifth paper of this series, did not permit the scoring of
either scale 5, the masculinity-femininity interest scale, or scale 0,
social introversion.) Later papers by Monachesi developed more com-

pletely the findings of Capwell and extended them to boys; a summary of these papers is included here to show the establishment of relationships between delinquency and some of the MMPI scales. In the last of the three papers demonstrating group differences between delinquents and nondelinquents, Ashbaugh applied the MMPI to adolescents in an entirely different environment and a somewhat different cultural setting. Lauber and Dahlstrom used the MMPI in studying the rehabilitation of delinquent girls. The last three papers of the series are devoted to our main interest in this field at present: namely, the analysis of early signs of delinquency in order to provide data for ultimately setting up better programs for the prevention of delinquency.

It is our hope that the results reported here will be a stimulus to the wider use of objective data in social agencies of all types and will incite others to extend and better these findings, which are undoubtedly crude in contrast to the potentialities for future development, both of analytic techniques that will improve the validity in the data and of better instruments. For the present at least, however, the MMPI appears to be one promising instrument for use in analyzing personality characteristics leading to juvenile delinquency.

THE MMPI

The MMPI is a psychometric instrument designed ultimately to provide, in a single test, scores on all the more clinically important phases of personality. In devising the instrument, the point of view determining the importance of a trait was that of a clinical or personnel worker who wishes to assay those traits commonly characteristic of psychological abnormality. The instrument itself comprises 550 statements covering a wide range of subject matter, from the physical condition of the individual being tested to his morale and social attitude. Subsequent experimentation has shown that it is also adapted to useful classification and understanding of "normal" persons.

For administration of the Inventory the subject is asked to respond to all statements, which are in the first person, as True, False, or Cannot Say. After he has so responded to all the items that he can as (mostly) True or (mostly) False about himself, his responses are counted so as to routinely yield scores on four validity scales and ten or more clinical scales. There are also a number of scales having special applications that are scored only when the implications of a given scale are applicable to the problem being evaluated in the subject. The time required for administration of the Inventory varies but is rarely longer than ninety minutes and is commonly as short as

thirty minutes. No supervision is needed beyond that required to let
the subject understand clearly the nature of his task and to assure
his optimal cooperation.

It is not possible here to give a complete description of MMPI
scales and their interpretation. The following is a brief review of the
most widely used scales and of coding and profile interpretation. The
literature on the MMPI and especially the *Atlas for the Clinical Use
of the MMPI* (37) should be consulted for a more complete background directly relating the patterns provided by the Inventory to
generalized concepts in the clinician so that he can form predictive
inferences. A brief study outline is also given here for the benefit of
those who have inadequate preparation.

As stated above, the MMPI is most commonly scored for fourteen
or more measures. Four of these are related to the accuracy and reliability of the subject's responses in the test, and the remaining ten
of the most widely used scales are related to various aspects of personality. These first four are often referred to as validity scores and
the ten others as clinical scales. All the scales are named with letters
and numbers rather than the longer diagnostic terms from which the
letters are partly derived. For example, a scale originally derived from
a study of schizophrenic patients is called "Sc," but this scale is better
referred to as scale 8 since it was the eighth scale that was derived for
clinical use. The diagnostic terms from which the scale names are
derived came from psychiatric practice and were applied to the scales
only because the clinical group on whom the scale was developed was
dominantly characterizable by the given term as usually employed.

Some of the papers included in this collection were written early in
the history of the development of the MMPI, and in those the longer
names of the scales appear more frequently than is true in the later
papers. For current usage it is better to refer to the clinical scales by
the numbers 0 to 9 rather than by letters, thus reminding the reader
that persons who obtain high scores on clinical scales should not
therefore be identified with mentally ill patients. The original use of
scales derived from patients grouped under the classificatory terms
used in psychiatric practice was not predicated on the assumption that
diagnostic categories are entirely reliable or stable or that these categories are pure ones; rather the argument in favor of these scales
rested upon the fact that the psychiatric syndromes of symptoms have
come to be widely accepted as having prognostic and internally cohe-
sive relationship and the nomenclature has an almost universal semantic standing.

MMPI SCALES

It is difficult to estimate how many variables will ultimately be needed to provide enough classes of behavior to allow for prediction of a wide variety of maladjustments, and yet not be so many as to exceed practical limits and make probability figures impossibly unreliable. The number of such variables would probably depend upon the degree of their intercorrelation and the pertinence of each to the various outcomes in which one might be interested. As seems to us apparent in the data presented in this collection of papers, the profiles provided by the MMPI are already so complex that large, though not impractical, numbers of cases are needed before useful and reliable prediction figures can be given. We feel that, although we were largely without foresight in the matter, this complexity is of approximately the right order. More complexity would leave us operating with little better than individuals, and less complexity would make the classes too inclusive to allow for the variety of outcomes.

The ? Scale

This score is obtained by counting the number of items in the Inventory that the subject did not answer (those he placed in the category Cannot Say). A high score would mean that, because so many items were left unanswered, no conclusions would be safe. Subjects are routinely urged to say True or False to nearly all the items.

The L Score

This little group of items yields a score tending to indicate any naive attempt on the part of the subject to put himself in a good light, chiefly with reference to personal ethics and social behavior. High scores are obtained on persons who try (often unconsciously) to answer all the items in ways that will seem to fit most clearly into the subject's interpretation of the moral code regardless of secret knowledge about himself to the contrary. Such attempts could be called defensiveness or, in more flagrant cases, "faking good."

The F Score

The F score is somewhat the opposite of the L score. Persons obtaining a high F score often seem to be attempting (perhaps unconsciously) to show themselves in a bad light. They may be "faking bad." Sometimes such persons are merely overly candid. This is called "plus getting" in MMPI jargon. The F score is also high if the subject, for any reason, fails to answer carefully or consistently; that is, one will obtain a high score for persons who cannot read well enough to make discriminative responses and, what is more significant for high school use of the Inventory, this scale will be high when the student answers carelessly, making random or facetious responses to the items. A third source of moderately high F scores is general maladjustment of a severe type.

The K Score

This variable is much more complex and less obvious than the L and F scores in its import. Special interpretation is not usually indicated because the score is mixed with five of the clinical scales in a way that properly uses the score as a correction. In general, higher K scores, like L but in a more subtle way, indicate defensiveness and lack of candor, and low K scores, like high F scores, indicate a degree of frankness and self-criticality.

The modification of scores on the five clinical scales by use of K was shown to be justified within the borderline abnormal score range. Routine use of K within the normal score range was not specially validated but is usually practiced to simplify application and interpretation.

Si, Scale 0

This is a measure related to social introversion and extroversion. Persons scoring high on the scale tend to hold back in personal inter-relationships and are likely to be socially seclusive. When the score is low, the individual is more extroverted, tends to join organizations with a primarily social purpose and to take an active part in them.

Hs, Scale 1

This scale was derived by comparison of normal persons to patients having many physical complaints with a preponderantly psychological basis. These complaints can be in part an outcome of obvious tissue pathology but are usually so varied and symbolic in nature that they are clinically classed with what is currently termed psychosomatic illness.

D, Scale 2

This scale was derived from persons who were depressed. Individuals obtaining a high score on it feel unsure of themselves and of the future and often they are sad and blue. Higher scores normally occur when the subject is in trouble and in a sense the absence of a higher score from a person in trouble is an unexpected sign since he seems not to be responding in the modal way.

Hy, Scale 3

This scale is closely allied to scale 1, but it is evidence of more complete symbolic elaboration of the physical symptoms. The elaboration usually takes the form of culturally respectable psychosomatic syndromes such as allergy or functional cardiovascular disturbances. The person with a high score on scale 3 defends the psychological elaborations against recognition of their neurotic character by himself or others. Persons who have high scores are more likely to avoid or run away from crises than to face them and work into them directly. In their avoidance of crises, they tend to try to adjust by "buck up" attitudes and when they are pushed too far, they develop physical or even psychological illness as a sort of solution.

Pd, Scale 4

The syndrome of symptoms that were characteristic of the patients from whom this important scale was derived is indicated by the diagnostic term *psychopathic deviate*. Often young and delinquent, these individuals always impress the clinician with their failure to be controlled by the ordinary mores of society. They seem little affected by remorse and do not appear to be particularly modified by censure or punishment. They are likely to commit asocial acts, but these frequently lack obvious motive.

It should not be assumed that all delinquents will score high on scale 4. The syndrome requires more than mere delinquency or criminality to establish the diagnosis. One may only be confident that any delinquent or criminal group will include an unknown number of persons who, if studied more broadly, would be so diagnosed. Youngsters who score high on scale 4 are more likely than adults to be in conflict with their families, but the social conflict can, of course, be more extensive.

Mf, Scale 5

This is a measure of masculinity or femininity of interests. In males, high scores are indicative of general feminine interests as these appear in contrast to the average male; in females, high scores indicate masculine interests. Persons who have homosexual tendencies often earn high scores; particularly is this true of males. High scores are not, however, safely interpreted in this way. This scale could not be scored on the early forms of the MMPI, and the earlier papers do not use it.

Pa, Scale 6

This scale is a measure of undue interpersonal sensitivity; at its extreme this may be a paranoid feeling about other people in which the subject feels mistreated or threatened. Probationers and other subjects under close social control are likely to show a moderate elevation of this score.

Pt, Scale 7

This scale is related to compulsions and obsessions. Persons with high scores are in some ways excessively meticulous or overly conscientious. This fussiness rarely characterizes all phases of a person's behavior, but tends to be most noticeable in restricted aspects. Others of those obtaining high scores worry more than is justified, while still others are overly introspective and self-critical. Some persons who senselessly repeat asocial acts are driven by compulsive energy. Arsonists, exhibitionists, and rapists are extreme cases likely to show this syndrome.

Sc, Scale 8

This is a measure related to the degree to which the person thinks and reacts like others about him. At the extremes, or with certain bizarre symptoms, the scale is an indicator of the mental disorder schizophrenia. More generally, the scale is a measure of the way in which the person may distort some aspects of the world about him, perceiving it differently than others and reacting to it in unusual ways.

Ma, Scale 9

This is a measure related to enthusiasm and energy. Persons scoring high on the scale become readily interested in things and approach problems with animation. When this becomes abnormal, the activity may lead to antisocial acts or to irrational manic behavior. Young people are normally characterized by a considerable amount of the factor this scale measures. When they have too much of it, they become restless and frequently stir up excitement for excitement's sake alone.

In addition to these, there are a number of other scales that have been developed to be scored on the MMPI. Undoubtedly some of the others will, in time, be as helpful as those outlined here. In the present collection, however, we shall restrict ourselves to findings with the scales described above.

THE MMPI PROFILE

In the summary presentation of MMPI data from a person, scores on the validity scales are usually given as simple raw scores. The ? score so frequently is low and satisfactory that it is not usually quoted. L, F, and K scores are quoted in that order. L scores of more than 5 are increasing evidence of defensiveness. A score of 10 or more is very high. F scores of 12 or more are considered fairly high, and a score of more than 18 is interpreted as rather severe evidence of invalidity or of maladjustment if other data indicate that the record is valid. K scores are average at 12 or 13. They clearly indicate defensiveness at 20 and higher. In the other direction, K scores of less than 10 represent more than usual candor, especially for young people.

The scores of the clinical scales are usually stated in what are referred to as T scores. These are standard scores derived from normal adults with the mean adjusted to 50 and the standard deviation adjusted to 10. A T score is larger as the scale indicates more abnormality. A T of 70 on a scale falls two standard deviations from the mean. Normal persons will show such scores on a given scale with a frequency of about 5 per cent. Other general rules for interpretation of T scores are hard to give since one must learn the characteristics of each scale in this regard.

After all scores are obtained on a record, they are indicated in order across a graph showing their relative size. This graph is called a "profile." The "high points" on such a profile are therefore the scales that show the largest T scores. If one or more T scores are as large as 70, the profile is usually considered to be elevated although not necessarily abnormal.

Although the MMPI scales are all arranged so that high scores indicate the usually recognized directions of personality abnormality, the extremely low score, statistically opposite to the high score, is often as useful a finding as is a high score. There is not much published information about these very low scores. In some cases it is indicated that they have interpretive significance usually related to problems of counseling or therapy. It is too simple and is unjustified by the clinical impressions of those who use the MMPI to assume that a low score on a given scale signifies a more normal person than average. On the contrary, it is probably better for the present to assume that an average score is the most normal score and that as a given score becomes lower and lower, some other factor than simple normality or the opposite of a given trait is the proper interpretation of the findings.

In description of profiles, the low scores tend to be emphasized by their competitive falling out of the high-score patterns. That is, we can characterize a profile by saying that scales 2, 3, or 5, or combinations of them, are the high points. In so characterizing the profile, it is implied that the other scores are lower, and the expressed pattern is obviously also dependent upon these lows, which are not specifically mentioned in the description of the profile.

CODING

The simplest way to encourage the reading of MMPI profiles with proper emphasis on the *pattern* of the scores rather than on the individual scores is to use codes. In this application, the word *code* refers to a method of expressing the profile in a simplified form which permits filing and reference work on the basis of the profile shape, or at least on the basis of salient features of the profile shape. For a complete treatment of the subject of coding, the reader should consult the *Atlas for the Clinical Use of the MMPI* or other references. The following is a brief outline and will suffice for some understanding of those papers in this volume which use codes for expressing the findings.

A code representing the clinical scales of an MMPI profile having one or more T scores at values greater than 54 always starts with the number of the scale on which the person has obtained his highest score. This scale number thus denotes the highest peak of the profile. Following this scale number in order are the numbers of all (if any) other scales for which the profile shows a score greater than 54. If T scores on any two of these scales are equal or within one point in size, they are underlined to show that they are interchangeable in position. When the profile being coded has a score or scores that exceed 70, the numbers of the scales representing such scores are separated from the rest of the code by a prime. (We sometimes use a double prime to separate at T score 80, a triple prime at 90, etc.) The completed series of scale numbers, representing in descending order the scores obtained by a person part of whose scores exceed 54, is called the high-point code.

For example, a high-point code might be written 9'4–. This means that for the profile in question two clinical scales had a larger T value than 54; one of them, the score for scale 9, was greater than 70. The score for scale 4 fell between 55 and 69 inclusive. The dash indicates the end of the high-point code.

As another example, the code '4<u>13</u>– would indicate that on the profile in question three scores were greater than 54 but none was as large as 70. Scale 4 was the highest with scales 1 and 3 somewhat lower and within one point equal in value. (This high-point code can be read equally correctly as '4<u>31</u>–.) The dash again indicates that the high-point code has ended. This therefore means that scores on all scales not in the high-point code had T values of 54 or less.

Complete coding includes the writing of a low-point code as well as a high-point code. To write the low-point code, one works from the lowest point of the profile. The numbers of scales are written following the dash of the high-point code in order as with the high-point code, except that the order now is determined by the ascending values. This process, beginning with the lowest point, is continued upward to include a T score of 45. When the ordered scale numbers that represent all scales with scores below 46 have been written, the low-point code is completed. Underlining is used as in the high-point code to indicate scores that are equal or within one point of one another. Sometimes a prime is used to separate scales below T score 40 analogously to the use of the prime at T score 70 in high-point codes.

A low-point code, for example, might read –2'90. The dash indicates the beginning of the low-point code and the 2 means that scale 2 was the lowest point of the profile. (When the prime is used as here, it shows that the scale 2 score was less than 40.) Scales 9 and 0 were at higher values but were still less than a T of 46. In the complete coding of a profile, scales having T scores among the values 46 to 54 inclusive are not specifically indicated in the code. These are the scores lying near the normal average for the scales (a T of 50) and are presumably less definitive than are the deviant scores that show in the high-point and low-point codes. It is understood in reading a code that scores not appearing in high-point or low-point codes are in this middle range represented by the dash.

A complete code with both high and low points might read 6'84–2<u>59</u>. This would be read as showing that scale 6 was above 70 in the profile, scales 8 and 4 were in the range of 55–69 inclusive, scales 2, 5, and 9 were below 46 with 2 lower than 5 and 9 which were equal or within one point of each other. Finally, this code shows that the remaining three scales (1, 3, and 7) had values in the range of 46 to 54 inclusive.

Only the clinical scales are coded in the high-point and low-point codes. Since, however, the validity scales are very important in the interpretation of a profile, these are usually given following the code. As the practice was established in the *Atlas for the Clinical Use of the MMPI*, the ? score is omitted under the assumption that it is satisfactory. No profiles with high Cannot Say scores are ever included in research data. On the other hand, L, F, and K values are always given and it is the practice to show these in raw score form following the code. Thus, if the code above were followed by the numbers 4,2,18, it should be understood that 4 was the raw score for L; 2 the raw score for F; and 18 that for K. T scores from these raw scores can be obtained by looking in the tables of the MMPI manual, although for the most part raw score values are utilized in evaluating these scales. In some instances where the L or F scores probably indicate unreliability of the whole profile, an X is inserted between the end of the code and the writing of the three raw scores for L, F, and K scales. This X merely calls attention to the large value of the L or F score, as the case may be.

One may arrange coded profiles according to shape as is done in the indexes of the *Atlas*. In that case the code is read as one would read letters in alphabetizing words. This permits the ready looking up of any code to compare with others having similar form. One should remember that underlined scale numbers should be looked up in all permutations.

PROFILE ANALYSIS

The interpretation of coded profiles obtained on the MMPI is best undertaken on the basis of profile analysis. By this we mean that the emphasis should not be upon the individual scores but rather upon the pattern of high and low scores seen as a profile.

The scales of the MMPI, as has been repeatedly emphasized, have their validity chiefly in relation to the usual patterns of adult mental disorder. There are few who would doubt that these patterns extend into the teen ages, and indeed most clinics see a considerable number of children who can be positively identified as experiencing a breakdown classifiable as we would classify similar disorders for adults. This is particularly true of the psychopathic deviate variety of psychopathic personality. In fact, the Pd scale of the MMPI was derived from a group of persons who, while all characterized by the diagnosis "psychopathic personality," were, in larger part than for any other validation group, young people of ages as low as 17 and 18. Nevertheless, it must be clearly emphasized that delinquency in children is not exclusively, in our opinion, to be related to the psychopathic or to neurotic or psychotic patterns. Rather the data here presented give some idea of the importance of those patterns among delinquent children without at this time developing other possible scales or classificatory systems.

The development of valid and useful information about a person from interpretation of his MMPI profile is complex and requires considerable clinical experience and familiarity with MMPI clinical reports. Elements of it, however, may be readily grasped. The four scales 1, 2, 3, and 7 are broadly related to what is clinically called neuroticism. Especially scales 1, 2, and 3 are referred to as the neurotic triad. Young people are not commonly deviants on these scales; and the presence of much depression, for example, or even of a high average adult amount of depression, is an indication of some trouble. Normal people, young and old, however, tend to become depressed and show high scale 2 values when they are in trouble or feel that they are rejected. When in a profile the scales of the neurotic triad are at higher values than other scales and when scales 1 and 3 are at larger values than scale 2 (codes beginning 132...) the resultant part of the profile is called "conversion V." This has been found to be common in immature persons who dodge issues rather than meeting them squarely.

Scales 6, 8, and 9 are derived from persons with severe psychological disorders and are indicators of relatively more definite trouble. Scales 4, 6, and 9 give indications that often relate to undesirable social behavior. (Apparently this adverse implication for scale 6 is not strong except when the T scores are above 70.) Particularly scale 4 is an indicator of asocial and amoral tendencies in young people.

The social introversion of scale 0 is frequently a social aspect of neuroticism as measured more definitively by scales 1, 2, or 7. Scale 0 is also allied clinically to scale 8 where social introversion is often tied closely to difficulties in personal intercommunication or to scale 6 where one finds that the person is socially introverted because he is suspicious of people or is easily hurt by what they say and thus withdraws from them. A low score on scale 0 is significant of social extroversion, and this is a fairly common feature of the active syndrome of high scale 9.

DELINQUENCY AND THE PROFILES

We do not know what to expect in the personality of the delinquent as reflected in the MMPI scales, except that from almost any routine interpretive approach high scores on scales 4 and 9 are the best indicators of delinquent tendencies. Very broadly speaking, preliminary

expectations as to treatment and possible outcomes could be sum-
marized by saying that when delinquency is related to neuroticism,
it is probably more easily treated in the individual and probably has
a better long-time prognosis. Second in threat to the future and difficulty of treatment would be those cases deviating on scales 4 and
9, the psychopath and hypomanic youngsters. Among such young
persons, age often seems to bring calmer and less obstreperous behavior. It is also probable that acceptable opportunities for useful
activity and rearrangement of environment will help such persons.
Least promising may be those delinquents who show a pattern related
to paranoid and schizophrenic trends. The more psychotic indicators,
scales 6 and 8, could presage continued trouble, although not necessarily repeated delinquency. For these persons we have fewer treatment approaches. On the other hand, very little is known about the
development and course of early psychotic trends. A very large number of persons having aberrant behavior characteristics get along fairly well in our society. To a certain extent we tolerate more readily
behavioral peculiarities when they occur in an older person. We are
prone to call the same acts that would incur only passing censure in
an adult, asocial or amoral if they attract our attention to an adolescent person, especially a girl.

Apart from the probable specific relationship of MMPI scales to
some cases of actual delinquency, there are certain generalities about
the scales that may apply to youth when contrasted to adulthood.
Young people are unquestionably more energetic and responsive to
excitement, and they are also probably more rebellious in various
ways than is the average middle-aged adult. These broad characteristics of youth would be expected to result in a higher average score on
scales 4, 6, and 9.

It might be maintained that such a contrast of the scores for youths
with those for adults is not fair and that scale norms should be considered in relation to adolescence and not to the average adult. There
are, however, adequate arguments against this adjustment of norms.
The culture only partially accepts the differences between youths and
adults. As an example, when young people express or use their energy
in ways that are acceptable to society, any differences implied in their
behavior are not censured or may be passed off by an attitude exemplified in the statement "Kids will be kids!" If, however, the exuber-
ance of youth produces acts that run counter to the interests or mores
of the adult, then such acts are regarded as evidence of a tendency to
delinquency and are labeled amoral or asocial. Essentially, this cul-

turally determined attitude can be summed up by saying that it is understood that young people are in need of excitement and are likely to be rebellious, but they are expected to hold these tendencies in check and express them within the limits considered proper by their parents or other adults.

In the light of this attitude, the application of adult norms to young people is proper and adjustment of the norms would obscure the very real fact that there is a significant, almost universal, quality in young people that makes them prone to socially unacceptable behavior. We want our scales to show behavior differences that are significant to society even if the implied personalities are "normal" for the age level. Since the core of society is the early adult and middle-aged pattern of mores, the use of MMPI norms based chiefly on middle-aged married persons can be justified even for young people.

MMPI STUDY PROGRAM

The best way to become familiar with the indications of the various profiles is to go through a course of study in the *Atlas*.* The case histories there are relatively unselected examples of patients having common types of profiles. In these moderately ill psychiatric patients, the characteristic symptoms stand out clearly, facilitating isolation and generalization by the reader. Naturally when one is trying to understand a less disturbed person who obtains a code similar to some with case histories detailed in the *Atlas*, he should expect milder symptoms and apply only the general characteristics. The ability to interpret profiles is much improved by practice.

As a course of study of the MMPI in the *Atlas* preparatory to better comprehension of studies on delinquency the following would be appropriate.

1. Become familiar with the arrangement of the *Atlas* as detailed in pages vii to xxi. Familiarize yourself with the indexes.

2. Read and attempt to identify the generalized characteristics of the following groups of selected case histories from the *Atlas*. After reading the indicated cases, read other less clear ones to try to detect the same tendencies as these appear mixed into complicated total problems.

*A recent publication, *The MMPI: A Review*, by William C. Cottle (Lawrence, Kansas: Kansas Studies in Education, University of Kansas Publications, vol. 3, no. 2, 1953), provides a review of many articles on the MMPI and a bibliography a little more up to date than that in the *Atlas*. It could profitably be used as a guide to further reading after this study program is completed.

1... Codes. Cases 12'3786–; 123'847–; 12386'7–; 12873'946– (*Atlas* pp. 16; 17–18; 19, 25–26).

These four cases are representative of the dominant hypochondriacal slant characteristic of high scale 1. Most of these cases in the *Atlas* are older and many have very elevated profiles with other extensive symptomatology. Profiles of cases with codes beginning 132... show the "conversion V" which is so characteristic of the syndrome P. Hys. Like similar cases with 312... these persons are likely to receive much medical attention from specialists. They are more likely to undergo surgical treatment than those in whose profiles scale 2 is equal to or greater than the values of scales 1 or 3.

31... Codes. Cases '31–47; '31–987; 312'48769–; 31'2684–9; 312'784–9; 312784'6–9; 3127'9486–; 314'892–; 31'48976–; 31'7982– (*Atlas* pp. 277; 278; 283–84; 290; 297–98; 298–99; 301; 312–13; 313; 316–17).

These cases show the general tendencies in symptoms when scale 3 is high. Most of the profiles show the "conversion V." Note the tendency for them to be younger than the 1... or 2... cases. Note particularly the much greater organization of symptomatic pictures around known types of organic illness. These persons are more likely to receive costly treatments or operations. Their illnesses often appear suddenly and can similarly be relieved suddenly by suggestion. As a group these individuals are more personally likable than are the other neurotic types.

2... Codes. Cases 217'386–; 23'47 861–9; 2'6973–; 276'138–9; 2786'41–9; 286'7341– (*Atlas* pp. 106; 135–36; 179–80; 221–22; 237–38; 254–55).

Here again, it is hard to find cases that are young since depression is much more a characteristic of older people. Also, most mentally ill persons react to their illness with depression; consequently high scale 2 profiles tend to be seen in patients who show complications of schizoid and other symptoms. It is difficult to find a person with "pure" depression.

7... Codes. Cases 7'2–148; 728'3–96; 7328416'–; 782'463–9; 7842'1936– (*Atlas* pp. 551–52; 559–60; 579; 591–92; 596).

These cases show the more extreme syndromes with 7... The persons who appear most ill are those with bizarre ideas. People who have compulsions, obsessions, or phobias are very common but are considered normal if the symptoms do not interfere seriously with their daily lives. When severe, the symptoms with 7... are usually closely allied to those with 8...

8... Codes. Cases 827'4–; 8'4172–; 84639'712–; 847'2639–; 84'769–13X;

8'672–3; 86'97234–; 89'4 137–6; 89'76–3 (*Atlas* pp. 616–17; 624; 627–28; 632–33; 634; 647–48; 657–58; 687; 690).

These cases show the real breaks of contact with reality that characterize the ill persons with 8... Here again, a great many individuals with 8... type profiles are not considered mentally ill. These may be referred to as unpredictable, seclusive, opinionated, or cranks, or by other descriptive terms, but society usually tolerates such aberration unless the individual becomes a danger to himself or others. Among still other normal persons with 8... there are those in whom the special and distinctive modes of thought are useful to society.

6... Codes. Cases '6–7893; '6327 841–X; 6'43879–; 64'97–1; 6'847–1; 68472'31–; 6847'239–; 6879'43–2; 6'98341–7 (*Atlas* pp. 497; 507–8; 516; 519–20; 527; 527–28; 528–29; 534–35; 545–46).

The symptoms of 6... are often very obvious but they can be so hidden that the problem is detectible only by means of the case history that contrasts with the normal role assumed by the person during an examination. Outstanding are irritability, oversensitivity to what others are thinking or saying, and a basic egocentricism at most only thinly veiled under an ostentatious self-depreciation.

9... Codes. Cases '9–26147; 9'4–26; 9'43–6712; 9'4678321–X; 9'48–237; 9'486–13; 9'8–2; 9'8–7; 9'8463–X; 98'467–2 (*Atlas* pp. 695; 712; 718–19; 721–22; 725; 730; 743–44; 745–46; 750–51; 751–52).

The symptoms of 9... are overactivity, restlessness, and need for excitement. When these are added to other syndromes such as 8 or 4 the combination is particularly likely to result in delinquent acts.

4... Codes. Cases '4–96; 423'8967–; 4'28–; 4'29–6; 43'829 761–; 46'–79; 4'63–; 46'829 37–; 46'83721–; 4'6938–7; 4'789–6; 4'79 286–1; 4'8193–; 4'8273–9; 4'83–; 487'2136– (*Atlas* pp. 359–60; 377–78; 387–88; 389–90; 400–1; 403–4; 408–9; 420–21; 422–23; 426; 434–35; 436; 443; 444–45; 449; 456).

More of these cases are given as typical because of their great importance in understanding this common pattern disposing to delinquency. Particular attention should be given by the reader to the aspects of the behavior that are not comprehensible as simpler motivated asocial behavior. The acts of the 4... person tend to be less understandable, for example, than stealing to get money, violence on the basis of provocation, or sexual excess on the basis of extra strong sexual desires; on the contrary these persons steal money when they have plenty, commit violence against persons who treat them well, and are sexually promiscuous although impotent or frigid.

3. Study Figures 1 to 8 in the *Atlas* emphasizing the changes in frequency of codes for the different populations and contrasting particularly the ninth-grade school children with others.

4. Similarly study Tables I to VIII with special reference to the school children.

5. Tables IX to XXVI are most important. Note especially Tables IX, X, XI, and XX. Persons of these types are more likely than others to be in trouble with the law.

Although the foregoing brief course of study will not prepare an untrained reader to interpret MMPI profiles authoritatively it will make the studies of this book more meaningful. In fact, we doubt that the book can make much contribution for readers without at least this much preparation.

Personality Patterns of Adolescent Girls: Delinquents and Nondelinquents

BY DORA F. CAPWELL

IN A STUDY devoted to the personality patterns of adolescent girls who show improvement in IQ (4) two groups of girls were used as subjects, a group of delinquents and a group of nondelinquents. A series of personality tests was administered to each group on two occasions along with tests of intelligence and academic achievement. The results of the personality tests are of special interest due to the degree and manner in which they differentiated the delinquents from the nondelinquents. Most present-day students of delinquency agree with the point of view expressed by Lowrey (40): "Delinquency is probably most frequently due to the subtle effects of interactions between individual and environment, leading to the establishment of particular personality sets." However, there has been disagreement regarding the success with which one can measure and delineate these personality sets by means of standard, objective tests of personality. The following results show the differences of personality between a group of delinquent girls and a group of nondelinquent girls as measured by one series of personality tests.

The procedure has been described in detail in the previous report (4). A total of 101 delinquent girls at the Minnesota State School for Girls and 85 nondelinquents in the public schools of Sauk Centre, Minnesota, were given a psychological examination and re-examined from 4 to 15 months later. The personality tests which were given twice were the Minnesota Multiphasic Personality Inventory (36), the Washburne Social Adjustment Inventory (55), and the Pressey Interest-Attitude Test (47). Two other tests of personality, the

EDITORS' NOTE. This paper has been reprinted, with slight modification, from the *Journal of Applied Psychology* for August 1945, by permission of the author and the editor of the *Journal*. The author is director of the Psychological Service of Pittsburgh, Pennsylvania.

Terman-Miles Test of Masculinity-Femininity (51) and the Vineland
Social Maturity Scale (12), were given just once. The levels of intelli-
gence and academic achievement were determined by the Kuhlmann
Tests of Mental Development (39) and the Stanford Achievement
Test (38).

RESULTS

Before examining the personality test results, it is important to note
the differences between the two groups in intelligence and achievement. The nondelinquents were girls of higher intelligence, showing a
mean IQ on the first test of 101, as compared with a mean of 87 for
the delinquents. The standard deviation for each group was 17. Each
group showed some retardation in school achievement when compared
with the norms of the Stanford Achievement Test. The delinquents
were more retarded than the nondelinquents, as would be expected,
but the differences are not statistically reliable. The amount of retardation in terms of grade scores is shown in Table 1.

The personality tests discriminated the delinquents from the nondelinquents with varying success; two of them showed striking differences. The significance of differences between the two groups on the
Minnesota Multiphasic Personality Inventory is shown in Table 2.

Each scale except the Hy, or hysteria scale, shows a clear differentiation between the two groups. The greatest difference appears in the
scores for Pd (psychopathic deviate). The extent to which the Multiphasic differentiated the groups may be seen in Table 3, and Figures
1 and 2 show graphically the differences in average T scores between
the two groups.

Table 4 shows the significance of differences between the raw scores
of the other personality tests. The Washburne and Vineland differentiated between the delinquents and nondelinquents, but the Pressey
Interest-Attitude and the Terman-Miles did not. On the Washburne
54 per cent of the delinquents reached or exceeded the 75th percentile
of the nondelinquents' scores on the first examination, and 51 per cent
did so on the second examination. The Vineland showed differences in
the other direction, in that on the other personality tests a high score
tends toward maladjustment, while on the social maturity scale a
high score is a favorable one. On the social maturity scale only 31 per
cent of the delinquents reached or exceeded the median of the nondelinquents.

Inasmuch as the two groups which were differentiated by the Multi-

TABLE 1. DIFFERENCE BETWEEN ACTUAL GRADE LEVEL AND ACHIEVEMENT GRADE SCORE OF DELINQUENT AND NONDELINQUENT GIRLS [a]

Score	Delinquents, N = 97 [b]		Nondelinquents, N = 85		D/σD between Delinquents and Non-delinquents
	Mean Diff.	SD	Mean Diff.	SD	
Total score	—1.30	1.41	—.82	1.50	2.28*
Reading score	—.55	1.52	—.49	1.46	.28
Arithmetic score	—1.96	1.76	—1.28	2.03	2.42*

* Difference significant beyond the 5 per cent level of confidence.
[a] 1.00 equals one total grade.
[b] Four delinquents were absent when these tests were given.

TABLE 2. MINNESOTA MULTIPHASIC PERSONALITY INVENTORY: SIGNIFICANCE OF DIFFERENCES BETWEEN RAW SCORES OF DELINQUENTS AND NONDELINQUENTS

Scale	First Test D/σD	Second Test D/σD
"?"	2.93**	4.25**
L	1.75	3.30**
F	7.21**	5.95**
Hs	3.11**	3.12**
D	4.59**	2.92**
Hy	2.74**	.60
Pd	16.00**	14.00**
Pa	12.00**	8.03**
Pt	6.64**	7.36**
Sc	7.10**	8.55**
Ma	8.00**	7.95**

** Difference significant beyond the 1 per cent level of confidence.

TABLE 3. PERCENTAGE OF DELINQUENTS WHO REACHED OR EXCEEDED THE 75TH PERCENTILE OF NONDELINQUENTS

Multiphasic Scale	Percentage of Overlap	
	First Test	Second Test
Hs	41	48
D	48	37
Hy	32	19
Pd	93	92
Pa	84	65
Pt	61	61
Sc	64	71
Ma	64	71

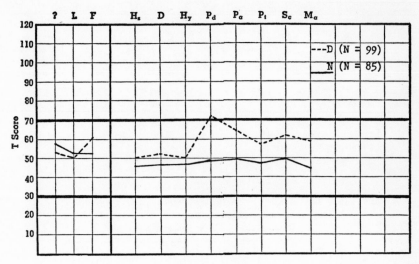

Figure 1. T Score Profile on the Multiphasic Inventory for the Delinquent (D) and Nondelinquent (N) Groups, First Test

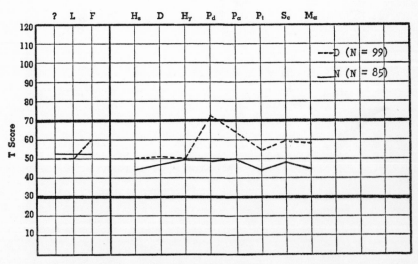

Figure 2. T Score Profile on the Multiphasic Inventory for the Delinquent (D) and the Nondelinquent (N) Groups, Second Test

TABLE 4. OTHER PERSONALITY TESTS: SIGNIFICANCE OF DIFFERENCES
BETWEEN RAW SCORES OF DELINQUENTS AND NONDELINQUENTS

Test	D/σD
Washburne	
First test	5.31**
Second test	4.54**
Pressey	
First test	.62
Second test	.61
Terman-Miles	.89
Vineland [a]	2.96**

** Difference significant beyond the 1 per cent level of confidence.
[a] D/σD between social quotients.

TABLE 5. MATCHED GROUPS OF DELINQUENTS AND NONDELINQUENTS:
SIGNIFICANCE OF DIFFERENCES OF RAW SCORES ON FIRST EXAMI-
NATION AND PERCENTAGE OF DELINQUENTS WHO REACHED OR
EXCEEDED THE 75TH PERCENTILE OF THE NONDELINQUENTS

Test	D/σD	Percentage of Overlap
Multiphasic		
Hs	1.95	..
D	3.91	55
Pd	10.34	93
Pa	8.43	84
Pt	4.86	57
Sc	4.06	57
Ma	5.22	63
Washburne	2.70	50
Vineland	.38	..

phasic, the Washburne, and the Vineland differ in level of intelligence
as well as in regard to delinquency, it is necessary to find out if the
personality test differences are related to the differences in intelligence.
Hence, 52 delinquents from the group were matched within two IQ
points with 52 of the nondelinquents in order to compare personality
differences and percentage of overlap on those tests which differentiated the groups reliably. The mean IQ of each group was 95 with a
standard deviation of 14. Only those tests were compared which differentiated the larger groups. Results obtained with the matched
groups may be seen in Table 5.

The Multiphasic continued to differentiate the delinquents and nondelinquents reliably with the exception of the Hs scale. Hy was not
used because it did not differentiate the larger groups. The Washburne

fell slightly below satisfactory reliability of differences, and the Vineland failed to demonstrate any real difference when the groups were matched for IQ. Hence, the differences on the Vineland appear to be related more to intelligence than to delinquency, but the differences on the Washburne and the Multiphasic continue to be significant.

DISCUSSION

The test which differentiated most clearly between these two groups was the Multiphasic. The results, which include the three validating scores, show first of all that even quite young adolescents do answer a well-devised personality inventory validly. The mean validity scores are close to a T score of 50 for all groups, except for the delinquent scores on the F scale; these were higher, but not sufficiently so as to invalidate the results. They would be expected to be somewhat higher than the F scores for the nondelinquents because of the much greater amount of maladjustment in the delinquent group, and because, as stated before, there is a slight tendency for the F score to be higher as gross maladjustment increases. The nondelinquents had many more "?" responses than the delinquents, probably because of two factors: first, they were a slightly younger group and found more items they did not understand, and, secondly, the delinquents had more leisure at the time of taking the tests. On the whole, however, the results from both groups showed a reassuring degree of validity.

It has long been believed that delinquents are more generally unstable than the normal population, and the Multiphasic Inventory bore out this belief by showing a significant difference of mean scores between delinquents and nondelinquents on seven of the eight scales, the delinquents scoring further away from the mean for the normal population. Even when the scores were not equivalent to a T score of 70 or over, the criterion for significant maladjustment, they still were further toward the maladjustment end of the scale than were the scores of the nondelinquents. The most conspicuous differences were on the scales of psychopathic deviate and paranoia. The delinquents had a mean T score of 73 on the Pd scale and 65 on the Pa scale.

The delinquents, on their arrival at a correctional institution, were not as depressed as one would imagine. That they were not is a finding which is consistent with the theory of the psychopathic deviate set forth by Hathaway (34), suggesting that the psychopathic inferior or deviate has trouble in his relations with society partly because he does not react with the emotions with which the normal person reacts under

similar circumstances. Therefore, although the newly committed delinquent may seem to feel very badly, cry noisily, and appear to be extremely depressed, the test scores and also the speed with which she
often recovers from this mood attest to the belief that it is a relatively
superficial emotion. In the nondelinquent group only two girls made
scores on the Pd scale as high as the mean for the delinquent group. Of
these two, one was a girl so maladjusted that she was being considered
for foster-home placement by the child welfare worker of the county,
and the other was a girl who had left school for a time, returned of her
own volition, but was again considering leaving and was so upset that
she was of concern to the school principal; she herself asked for a con-
ference with the examiner to talk about her difficulties. Thus, this test
measures adjustment in the same sense in which nondelinquents are
better adjusted than delinquents.

Two other personality tests, the Pressey Interest-Attitude Test and
the Terman-Miles Test of Masculinity-Femininity, when their raw
scores were compared as with the other tests, did not discriminate
between the delinquents and nondelinquents. This is contrary to the
results implied by the report of Durea and Fertman (14), who gave
the Pressey to 180 delinquent girls. Their study merely showed, however, that the scores from the delinquents compared "unfavorably
with norms for non-delinquents." No control group was used at the
same time. In the present data the delinquents compare unfavorably
with the *norms,* but so does this particular sample of normal cases.
These same normal girls made normally expected scores on the other
tests. The Pressey apparently does not measure the type of adjustment measured by the Multiphasic or the Washburne. The Terman-
Miles did not show significant differences between the groups, but
each group contained some cases of extreme scores, as one may judge
from the standard deviation of the groups. The deviate cases were not
always the girls who tested as most maladjusted on other tests.

The Vineland Social Maturity Scale did not show as much difference
in social maturity as might be expected between the delinquents and
nondelinquents. These girls do not show as much social retardation as
the delinquent boys reported by Doll and Fitch (12), but there are
other marked differences between the boys they studied and the girls
of this study, the most important one being that the boys were much
more retarded mentally than the girls are. The median mental age for
the boys was 9.3 years, as against a median life age of 14 years. The
social quotients were nearer the mental ages than the life ages. In the

present group of delinquent girls the mean social quotient is 4 points below the mean IQ and is more related to intelligence level than delinquency.

In concluding the discussion of these test results a word may be said about the use of personality tests as measures of adjustment both with groups and individuals. Whether or not one considers them valid and helpful instruments to aid diagnosis appears to depend largely on the selection of tests one uses. Boynton and Walsworth (3) used six tests, all different from the ones used in the present study, with 47 delinquent and 50 normal girls and found that only one score of one test yielded a C.R. of 3.00 between the groups. They concluded that the tests "in the main do not provide empirical evidence of sufficient validity to justify one in putting a great deal of faith in them in individual and group diagnosis." They concluded further that since there was such disparity between the test results, delinquent behavior is not necessarily associated with personality aberrations.

Somewhat different conclusions are warranted from the results of tests used in the present study. Two of them, the Terman-Miles M.-F. Test and the Pressey Interest-Attitude Test, were not helpful in differentiating delinquents and nondelinquents. Two others, however, gave satisfactory differences and should be helpful in either individual or group diagnosis; these two were the Minnesota Multiphasic Personality Inventory and the Washburne Social Adjustment Inventory. The results of both suggest that personality aberrations frequently *are* associated with delinquency. The use of personality tests with any special group necessitates careful selection of tests on the basis of the way they were standardized as well as their suitability for providing the desired information. Beyond that, experience with the results in the particular group concerned is necessary before a fair evaluation can be made of the usefulness of the test. Generalization from a selected group of personality tests to all tests of that type is not warranted any more than from one intelligence test to another.

SUMMARY AND CONCLUSIONS

A group of 101 delinquent and 85 nondelinquent girls were tested with a battery of personality tests and retested from 4 to 15 months later. Differentiation between the two groups was measured by computing the significance of difference of the mean scores for each group and also the percentage of overlap. The groups differed in level of intelligence as well as in delinquent tendencies, so the effect of mental level on the personality test scores was investigated by similar statistical treatment of the scores of 52 girls from each group who were matched for IQ. The results led to the following conclusions:

1. The Minnesota Multiphasic Personality Inventory and the Washburne S.-A. Inventory discriminated the delinquents from the nondelinquents in degree of personality adjustment.

2. The Vineland Social Maturity Scale showed differences which were more related to intelligence than to delinquency.

3. The Pressey Interest-Attitude Test and the Terman-Miles Test of Masculinity-Femininity did not discriminate the delinquents and nondelinquents.

4. Personality tests may be of value with individuals or groups in measuring and describing the personality patterns of delinquent as distinguished from nondelinquent girls.

The Personality Patterns of Juvenile Delinquents as Indicated by the MMPI

BY ELIO D. MONACHESI

THE discriminatory capacity of the MMPI, when applied to delinquent and nondelinquent girls, was demonstrated for the first time in a study published in 1945 by Dora F. Capwell (5, also Study 1). She reported that most of the scales reliably differentiated the two groups. Except for scale L and scale 3 (Hy) on the second test, the delinquent girls had reliably larger mean T scores on clinical scales. These differences suggested that the delinquents were more maladjusted. When a selected group of 52 delinquent girls was matched on IQ with 52 nondelinquent, the differentiation was still reliable except on scale 1 (Hs); thus the differences in mean scores on the scales seemed not related to measured intelligence.

Capwell did not use scale 5 (Mf), nor did she use the suppressor scale K. On validity scales L and F, her delinquent girls obtained reliably different scores indicating less defensiveness; they obtained a lower mean score on L and a higher mean score on F. Later scoring of her records showed the mean K of her delinquents to be about equal to the adult mean, but the mean of her nondelinquent girls was above that of the adult norm group.

The Capwell results were of sufficient importance to warrant attempts to find out whether the instrument would continue to differentiate between delinquent and nondelinquent girls and whether it would also differentiate between delinquent and nondelinquent boys. The following studies were made with these questions in mind.

Early in 1946 the MMPI was administered to 128 delinquent boys and girls. These delinquents were found in Hennepin County and Ram-

EDITORS' NOTE. This paper is a summary and synthesis of three articles published in 1948 and 1950 in the *Journal of Criminal Law and Criminology* (42, 43, and 44) and two unpublished articles. The data are used by permission of the editor of the *Journal*.

sey County home schools and were tested with the booklet form of the Inventory. To obtain enough cases it was necessary, however, to test some delinquents who were on probation in the same communities; thus the delinquents of this sample are heterogeneous in that about half were actual prisoners and the remainder were on probation when tested. Arbitrarily, and possibly overconservatively, any profile was omitted from the data of these studies that showed an L or an F score equal to or greater than a T score of 70. With this criterion, L raw scores above 9 and F raw scores above 11 were deemed unacceptable. After omission of these questionable profiles, there remained of the 1946 delinquent samples two groups of valid profiles made up of 48 delinquent girls and 49 delinquent boys.

In 1947 an additional group of delinquent girls was tested. This sample, made up of 60 girls from whom 47 valid records were obtained, was a repetition of the sampling of 1946 except that these girls were wholly from Ramsey County. These 1947 girls were again either prisoners or on probation.

The 1946 and 1947 testing in the county home schools resulted, therefore, in two samples of delinquent girls and one of delinquent boys. To obtain a second sample of delinquent boys who were more likely to show extreme behavior deviation, the MMPI booklet form was administered to 123 male delinquents confined in the Minnesota State Training School at Red Wing. These were all the boys 13 years old or older who were not in the disciplinary company or the hospital on the day when the test was administered. After 43 of the obtained records were discarded on the basis of the validity criteria specified above, there remained 80 cases with suitable profiles which will hereafter be referred to as the training school sample.

To provide comparative data against which the four samples of delinquents might be contrasted, two samples each of presumably nondelinquent boys and girls were obtained. The first samples, consisting of valid profiles from 56 nondelinquent boys and 79 nondelinquent girls, were obtained in 1946. In an attempt to equate socioeconomic status with that of the delinquents, these two nondelinquent samples were obtained among groups whose members were drawn chiefly from neighborhoods similar to those from which the delinquent youngsters in county home schools came. The samples included Girl Reserves, Girl Scouts, Boy Scouts, boys in a settlement house recreational club, boys from a Hi-Y group, and both boys and girls from among the students in two high school classes.

In order to obtain two additional nondelinquent samples from families in upper socio-economic classes, the students in a denominational academy were later tested. This academy is located in one of the better residential sections of Minneapolis, and its student body is recruited for the most part from the Twin Cities. Tuition is high enough to exclude most youths who belong to lower income classes. The academy sample yielded 123 valid male profiles and 233 valid female profiles. Analysis of the occupational status of the fathers indicated that 71 per cent of those in the academy samples belonged to the professional, semiprofessional, and other classes down to skilled occupations. This percentage contrasted with 24 per cent in these classes for fathers of the 1946 nondelinquent samples and 16 per cent for fathers of the delinquents.

Of all the samples, delinquent and nondelinquent, the delinquent boys and girls thus came from the lowest socio-economic background, although the difference was not great between them and the 1946 nondelinquent samples of boys and girls. At the top of the socio-economic scale are the two academy samples, which will be referred to as the academy boys and the academy girls.

In general, it is also to be kept in mind that the IQ's of the delinquents were lower on the average than were those for the nondelinquents. For example, the median IQ of the 1946 delinquent boys was 101 and that of the 1946 nondelinquent boys was 109. The median IQ of the 1946 delinquent girls was 103 and that of the nondelinquent girls 108. (Although IQ data were available for the academy samples, they were collected with tests different from those utilized in testing the other groups and therefore are not comparable.)

The academy boys were the oldest on the average. The median age of the 1946 delinquent boys was 15.5 years, and the median age of the 1946 nondelinquent boys was 15.9. The training school age median was 16.1. The academy girls had a median age of 16.0, the 1946 delinquent girls a median age of 16.3, and the 1946 nondelinquent girls a median age of 16.4. The 1947 delinquent girls had a median age of 16.6. The academy boys were a little older with a median age of 16.9.

In summary, MMPI profiles from four groups of boys and four groups of girls are available for analysis. All these profiles were rather rigorously selected for validity according to the ?, L, and F scales of the MMPI. There are two samples of delinquent boys, 49 in county detention homes or on probation and 80 in the training school. There are also two samples of delinquent girls, the 1946 sample and the 1947 sample consisting of 48 and 47 girls respectively. These samples were similar in general selection factors.

There are four groups of presumptively nondelinquent cases available for contrast to these delinquent samples. These are referred to as presumptively nondelinquent since no check was made to determine for certain that they had not been delinquent or did not at the time have personality characteristics like those of youngsters known to be in trouble. The only known fact about them was that they were not publicly in difficulty with the law. The first two nondelinquent samples were obtained from organized groups of boys and girls and consisted of 56 boys and 79 girls tested at the time of the 1946 testing of delinquents. Later, boys and girls from a private school were tested yielding valid profiles from 123 boys and 223 girls. In socio-economic status, all the delinquent groups were somewhat below the 1946 nondelinquent samples and definitely below the two academy samples. In IQ the delinquent samples were also lower and the academy samples probably highest. In age all the samplings were rather similar at around the median age of 15 or 16 years.

RESULTS

Tables 1 and 2 give comparative data for the various samples. The reliable differences between the nondelinquent samples on L are not large enough to have much interpretive significance, but they and the less reliable differences on K indicate more defensive answers from both sexes of the academy sample. In this connection, Hathaway and Meehl (41) suspected that the K factor was related to socio-economic status. This was confirmed by Perlman (46). The present data are in accord with this hypothesis since the academy sample came from the highest socio-economic level. On the clinical scales, the boys of the two nondelinquent groups show no significant differences in means. There is a tendency for the academy boys to have mean scores a little closer to adult normal means (T score 50). The academy girls obtain mean scores on scales 5 and 6 that are reliably different from the 1946 nondelinquents above the 5 per cent level of confidence. These differences on scales 5 and 6 indicate that the academy girls are slightly more masculine (Mf) and a little less sensitive to personal references (Pa).

Since the mean T scores for adult normals as observed in the norm groups for the MMPI are 50 (there is some difference from this for scales where male and female norms are combined), the nondelinquent

		Means			Difference between Means	
					1946 Nonde-	
Scales	1946 Non-delinquent Boys, N = 56	Academy Boys, N = 123	1946 Delin-quent Boys, N = 49	Training School Boys, N = 80	linquents minus Academy Group	1946 Delin-quents minus Training School Group
L 54		55	56	54	—1 **	2
F 60		58	60	60	2	0
K 51		53	55	52	—2	3
1 (Hs) + .5K 53		54	56	54	—1	2
2 (D) 52		51	57	55	1	2
3 (Hy) 53		54	57	54	—1	3
4 (Pd) + .4K 61		59	68	72	2	—4 *
5 (Mf) 54		54	53	53	0	0
6 (Pa) 56		53	58	60	3	—2
7 (Pt) + 1K 59		57	56	61	2	—5 *
8 (Sc) + 1K 62		60	63	65	2	—2
9 (Ma) + .2K 61		59	58	62	2	—4 *

*Signifies a difference reliable above the 5 per cent level of confidence.
**Signifies a difference reliable above the 1 per cent level of confidence.

		Means			Difference between Means	
					1946 Nonde-	
Scales	1946 Non-delinquent Girls, N = 79	Academy Girls, N = 223	1946 Delin-quent Girls, N = 48	1947 Delin-quent Girls, N = 47	linquents minus Academy Group	1946 Delin-quents minus 1947 Delin-quents
L 54		56	54	54	—2 *	0
F 56		55	61	58	1	3 *
K 54		56	51	53	—2	—2
1 (Hs) + .5K ... 50		51	54	50	—1	4
2 (D) 49		49	54	54	0	0
3 (Hy) 52		53	55	54	—1	1
4 (Pd) + .4K 58		58	77	69	0	8 **
5 (Mf) 51		54	56	57	—3 *	—1
6 (Pa) 55		53	66	57	2 *	9 **
7 (Pt) + 1K 55		56	59	55	—1	4 **
8 (Sc) + 1K 58		56	65	58	2	7 **
9 (Ma) + .2K ... 56		56	61	58	0	3

*Signifies a difference reliable above the 5 per cent level of confidence.
**Signifies a difference reliable above the 1 per cent level of confidence.

samples of boys and girls all show some definite differences from adults. The differences are most marked for scales 4, 6, 7, 8, and 9. Using common adjectives for the clinical implications of these scales, they indicate the youngsters to be comparatively rebellious (scale 4), personally sensitive (scale 6), obsessive-compulsive (scale 7), apart or detached in affect and concept formation (scale 8), and active with impulsiveness (scale 9). Certainly some of these indications are reasonable enough if one considers the contrasts between the behavior of adolescents and that of mature adults.

The significance of these scores for the present analysis lies in the fact that comparisons of delinquent adolescents with nondelinquent adolescents will show much less difference than would be true if one compared juvenile delinquents with a general sample of adults. The reader should keep this fact in mind. We expect youths to get into some trouble from rebellion and overactivity. It may be presumed that youths not observed to be delinquent are, as a descriptive group characteristic, more prone to behavior difficulties of the types found among the delinquents than would be true of adults. In tendency toward exuberant vandalism and sexual promiscuity, youth is insurgent and held under control by the cultural mores and institutions with special difficulty.

One may assume, therefore, that the differentiations between *known* offenders and nondelinquents as measured by a personality test would be attenuated. Unselected samples of youths who happen not to have been apprehended as delinquent should a priori be measurably different from adults on scales that measure traits characteristic of adolescence. Culturally we tend to disregard the differences by comparing youths only to other youths. The degrees of increased rebellion contributing to apprehension and conviction as a delinquent could hardly be expected to show sharply by any measurement against unselected samples of the same population.

In the two delinquent male groups of Table 1, the training school boys show a tendency to obtain reliably higher scores on scales 4, 7, and 9. As a group, the training school boys would presumably be more severely delinquent and this finding seems a reasonable one for 4 and 9 of these three scales. The scale 7 difference is less to be expected. Although the differences are not reliable, the 1946 delinquent sample of boys obtains higher scores on the neurotic triad (scales 1, 2, and 3).

Table 2 shows the means and differences in means of the two samples of delinquent girls. These differences, all of which are one or more times the standard deviation of the groups, occur on scales 4, 6, 7, and 8. There is also a reliable difference on F although the absolute size of this difference is not so great. The four significant differences are in a direction indicating the 1947 delinquent girls to have less severe behavior disorder trends on the average.

As a hypothesis to explain this difference, one can readily imagine that the general characteristics of the two delinquent groups might have been different through variations in court procedure. The 1947 sample was obtained from Ramsey County, the 1946 cases about equally from Ramsey and Hennepin counties. In the absence of standard procedures and standard measuring and estimation of cases handled by the courts, it is not unreasonable to expect that at one period of time the average girl sent to a detention home should have a less severe personality deviation than the average girl committed at another time. Public pressure, for example, tends to determine the action of the police and the courts, at one time encouraging the severe treatment of minor deviations so that girls are sent to detention homes quite freely and readily, whereas at another time an opposite trend may be dominant and the group ending up in detention homes may represent only the severe cases. It is difficult to establish the extent of such variations in disposition of cases, but the existence of such variations is not questioned by most persons who have experience in the field.

Another hypothesis to account for this difference could be based upon the lower F and higher K scores obtained by the 1947 girls. These mean differences, if they are stable, could be related to a difference in test-taking attitude, with the 1947 girls more on the defensive. Such defensiveness could have resulted from differences in examination conditions. The examiner or other conditions of the test situation may have made the 1946 girls feel more secure and generally more ready to cooperate frankly.

In any case, whatever may be the explanation, the 1947 group of delinquent girls showed less measured maladjustment than did the 1946 sample.

All four of the delinquent groups show clearly significant differences from average adult norms. If we are interested in establishing the existence of measurable differences between the average adult and the nondelinquent adolescent or the average adult and the delinquent adolescent, then these differences seem clear on most of the scales; the more marked differences are those between the adult and the adolescent delinquent, with the nondelinquent youngster in the middle.

Table 3 shows the various comparisons of the delinquent with the nondelinquent samples of boys and girls. Among boys there is a tendency for L and K scores to show differences in the direction indicating greater guardedness on the part of the delinquent groups. There is also a tendency for the delinquent boys in both the 1946 and the training school samples to appear more depressed. This scale 2 difference is largest for the 1946 delinquent group, which had a mean score on this scale of 57. Possibly depression is more marked among boys who are in the less stable situation of probation or detention home than is true for groups from the relatively stable population of the training school. In the same connection, overactivity (scale 9) is less in the 1946 sample of delinquents than in any of the other three samples of boys (see Table 1). The slightly more neurotic character of the 1946 delinquent group of boys is also exemplified in scales 1 and 3 which, with scale 2, make up the neurotic triad of the MMPI. In some contrast to this finding, the Pt scale, which is also often allied with neuroticism, shows a lower mean for the 1946 delinquents than for the other groups; but this is more understandable when one notes that the mean on scale 7 for the 1946 delinquents is much higher than the norm for the adults.

The finding relative to scale 4 is in distinct support of the assumption that delinquent groups include many persons similar to clinical cases receiving the diagnosis psychopathic personality, asocial and amoral type. The psychopathic deviate patient as seen clinically is most frequently young and delinquent. Significant and reliable differences show up on scale 4 for all the comparisons. As one would expect, the differences are larger when the training school boys are compared with nondelinquent groups. In evaluating the size of these differences we must again remind ourselves that the nondelinquent groups have scores on scales 4, 7, 8, and 9 that are clearly above those of the average adult; and there is good reason to think that many nondelinquent youths are close to at least mild open revolt or delinquent behavior.

Among the differences between the groups of girls, the validity scores show a definite tendency in the direction of less defensiveness for the delinquent samples. This is evidenced by a lower L and a significantly lower K together with a significantly higher F score. Capwell also found a lower L score and higher F score among her delin-

TABLE 3. DIFFERENCES IN MEAN T SCORES BETWEEN DELINQUENT AND NONDELINQUENT GROUPS

Scales	Boys[a]				Girls[b]			
	1946 Delinquents minus 1946 Nondelinquents	1946 Delinquents minus Academy Group	Training School Group minus 1946 Nondelinquents	Training School Group minus Academy Group	1946 Delinquents minus 1946 Nondelinquents	1946 Delinquents minus Academy Group	1947 Delinquents minus 1946 Nondelinquents	1947 Delinquents minus Academy Group
L	2*	1	0	-1	0	-2	0	-2*
F	0	2	0	2**	5**	6**	2	3*
K	4*	2	1	-1	-3*	-5**	-1	-3*
1 (Hs) + .5K	5*	6**	3	0	4*	3	0	-1
2 (D)	5*	3*	3	4*	5*	5*	5**	5**
3 (Hy)	4*	1	1	0	3**	2	2	1
4 (Pd) + .4K	7**	9**	11**	13**	19**	19**	11**	11**
5 (Mf)	-1	-1	-1	-1	5*	2	6**	3*
6 (Pa)	2	5**	4*	7**	11**	18**	2	4**
7 (Pt) + 1K	-3	-1	2	4*	4**	3**	0	-1
8 (Sc) + 1K	1	3	3	5**	7**	9**	0	2
9 (Ma) + .2K	-3	-1	1	3*	5**	5**	2	2

* Signifies a difference reliable above the 5 per cent level of confidence.
** Signifies a difference reliable above the 1 per cent level of confidence.
[a] 1946 delinquent boys' N = 49; 1946 nondelinquent boys' N = 56; male academy group's N = 123; training school group's N = 80.
[b] 1946 delinquent girls' N = 48; 1946 nondelinquent girls' N = 79; female academy group's N = 223; 1947 delinquent girls' N = 47.

quent girls. Furthermore, although Capwell did not use K, a later scoring of her records showed her reform school girls to have an average K score three points lower than the control group mean. As in the present case, the control group K score was high and the delinquents came closer to the adult average.

That test-taking attitude is an important factor in these measurements is indicated by comparison of these validity scores with those of the boys. The boys showed an opposite trend, with the delinquents appearing more defensive. Since reference to Table 2 shows that the mean K score for the nondelinquent girls is relatively high, compared to the normal adult 50, one might say that there is a tendency for nondelinquent girls to be relatively defensive and to "cover up" as a reaction pattern. This defense pattern seems to weaken with delinquency, or perhaps delinquent girls did not have it in the first place.

In this and other studies showing MMPI scale averages on delinquents in contrast to nondelinquents, the differentiation between the two groups on scales that are K corrected is in some comparisons less reliable statistically than if the K correction were omitted (Table 4).

TABLE 4. SIGNIFICANCE OF DIFFERENCES (CRITICAL RATIOS) BETWEEN DELINQUENT AND NONDELINQUENT BOYS AND GIRLS OF THE 1946 SAMPLES AS THEY ARE AFFECTED BY THE K CORRECTIONS

Scale	Boys[a] (K is 2.48)		Girls[b] (K is 2.12)	
	K Corrected	Uncorrected	K Corrected	Uncorrected
1 (Hs)	1.40	−.25[c]	2.28	3.49
4 (Pd)	3.98	2.84	9.61	10.55
7 (Pt)	−1.26	−2.85	3.12	5.18
8 (Sc)	.20	−1.72	3.85	4.96
9 (Ma)	−1.58	−2.13	3.33	2.82

[a] Delinquent boys' N = 49; nondelinquent boys' N = 56.
[b] Delinquent girls' N = 48; nondelinquent girls' N = 79.
[c] Minus signs indicate differences with delinquent means smaller.

One may not conclude from this that the K correction is an improper one. In the research that led to the development of the K correction, the intent was to establish maximum validity of the scale for determining the clinical entity psychopathic deviate. Psychopathic deviate is a subtype among those patients commonly called psychopathic personality in the regular terminology. But this clinical syndrome is not likely to be the only one observed among delinquent children. These general delinquents are known to have behaved in ways that are undesirable from a social standpoint, and many psychopathic deviate cases as seen clinically have misbehaved in similar ways. But the diagnosis of psychopathic deviate is not dependent merely upon this misbehavior. Such a diagnosis can be arrived at only in view of other classical symptoms of the disorder.

It may well be, then, that the K correction helps in the selection of those particular delinquent cases where the clinical diagnosis of psychopathic deviate is appropriate, while tending to decrease the differentiation of other delinquents from the general adolescent population. The observation that any K corrected scale is diminished in its capacity to discriminate delinquency by the K correction does not constitute evidence that the K correction is inappropriate for the clinical purposes of the scale. This could only be done in these five scales as it was done in the original studies deriving the K corrections themselves: namely, by the study of properly diagnosed cases that are known to have many aspects of the clinical syndromes.

If one were intent solely on increasing mean difference reliabilities between delinquent and nondelinquent groups, it would be desirable to omit the K correction. If this is done, the validities of the noncorrected scales are changed from their original clinical ones toward the discrimination of delinquency. This could be a permissible intent; and if no generalization to other clinical syndromes is implied, then the K correction can be omitted. A study designed to detect delinquency would probably not use the K correction; but if in presenting the results of such a study, the issue of the frequency of psychopathic deviate as a clinical entity or of hypochondriasis or of any of the other three clinical syndromes should be discussed, then K corrected scores must be used until evidence based on a properly studied and diagnosed sample of patients is brought forth that establishes the correction as inappropriate.

Among the clinical scales, scale 2 (depression) shows a significant and reliable difference, the delinquent group being more depressed. It would seem reasonable enough to relate this to lowered defenses and to accept the tentative hypothesis that, in contrast to boys, girls who are in detention homes or on probation are on the average more candid and have more insight than nondelinquent girls.

Of other clinical scale differences among the girls, the neurotic triad of scales 1, 2, and 3 shows a tendency to be higher among the 1946 delinquents when they are compared with nondelinquents. However, it appears more likely that any elevation of the whole neurotic pattern is related to the depression evidenced by scale 2 rather than to basic neuroticism of a more general sort. Depression, from whatever source, is usually related to a moderate increase of general neuroticism. At any rate, if there is such a trend, the 1947 delinquents (who are a little more defensive) do not show it convincingly.

As is to be expected, scale 4 again shows outstanding differential strength; and all four comparisons show significant separation of the groups. Scale 9 is not so strong, but the tendency is marked; particularly the 1946 delinquent girls were, according to this scale, more hyperactive and ready to "stir up some excitement." The 1946 group also shows a strong differentiation on scales 6 and 8, with scale 6 being the outstanding one. This combination is clinically related to paranoid and schizoid types of personality. One might not expect these persons to make up a large proportion of delinquent cases, who would seem as a class more likely to fall into other types of maladjustment. Capwell also found distinct elevations on these scales for her girls; and it is highly possible that maladjusted girls, when that maladjustment is of the rebellious, detached sort, are more likely to be sent to detention homes or to a reform school than are boys having the same pattern of behavior. If such tendencies on the part of the authorities were operating to make the 1946 and the Capwell samples of delinquent girls more often of this disturbed sort, something must have operated differently in the 1947 delinquent girls since the trend, while present, is much less reliable.

The fact that 45 per cent of the training school delinquents had been committed by courts outside of the major urban areas of Minnesota makes possible a comparison of boys from urban areas with those from rural areas. Courts in rural areas seldom have the treatment facilities provided for urban courts. A lack of varied treatment and placement possibilities might result in the commitment of less disturbed delinquents who would have been given another type of treatment had such facilities been available. This would make the average maladjustment of delinquents committed from rural areas seem less.

Table 5 shows the mean scores of metropolitan contrasted with non-metropolitan boys. Scales 1 and 3 are reliably larger for the metropolitan boys and throughout there is an unmistakable tendency for the metropolitan group to show more maladjustment. These data would be consistent with the hypothesis above that the metropolitan boys committed to the training school are selected to be a little more maladjusted than are the rural cases. Rural courts may, therefore, be more prone to send a less disturbed boy to the training school, having little alternative in the community. There may be some preliminary, objec-

tive evidence here of the value of adequate rural probation and other
social treatment facilities in cutting down on the number of youths
who are committed.

Much has been said about the part played by broken homes in the
development of personality and behavior difficulties of children. Nu-

TABLE 5. MEAN T SCORES FROM METROPOLITAN AND NONMETROPOLITAN
DELINQUENT BOYS

| | Mean Scores | | |
Scales	Metropolitan Group, N = 44	Nonmetropolitan Group, N = 36	Difference in Mean Scores
L	54	55	−1
F	61	60	1
K	52	53	−1
1 (Hs) + .5K	56	51	5 *
2 (D)	56	53	3
3 (Hy)	56	51	5 **
4 (Pd) + .4K	74	70	4
5 (Mf)	53	52	1
6 (Pa)	60	59	1
7 (Pt) + 1K	62	59	3
8 (Sc) + 1K	66	63	3
9 (Ma) + .2K	64	61	3

* Signifies a difference reliable above the 5 per cent level of confidence.
** Signifies a difference reliable above the 1 per cent level of confidence.

merous reports from many sources indicate that delinquent children
are more probably from broken homes than otherwise. The county
home girls and the girls on probation in the 1946 and 1947 samples of
delinquent girls were available for some comparison of a broken home
group with a group in which the home had remained together. There
were 53 girls from broken homes and 49 from unbroken homes. Table
6 shows the mean scores and differences between these two groups.

On the whole, the differences show a marked tendency for the broken
home group to be more maladjusted. There are only two scales in which
this is reversed. Scale 2, measuring depressive trends, shows a tendency
to be higher in the unbroken home group, although this tendency is
not very reliable. Scale 7 shows a more reliable tendency to be higher
for the unbroken home group. It could be assumed that girls from unbroken homes are more deeply affected by getting into trouble with
the law and react to it in two of the more normal psychological ways
among neurotic reaction types: namely by depression and by brood-
ing, the obsessive-compulsive tendency of scale 7. As further evidence

consistent with this hypothesis, the K scale shows a somewhat greater defensiveness among the unbroken home girls.

The whole pattern of these three differences in mean score could be regarded as a reaction in which the delinquent child from an unbroken home reflects a deeper concern and appreciation for the trying position

TABLE 6. MEAN T SCORES MADE BY DELINQUENT GIRLS FROM
BROKEN AND UNBROKEN HOMES

	Mean Scores		
Scale	Broken Home Group, N = 53	Unbroken Home Group, N = 49	Difference in Mean Scores
L	56	54	2
F	60	58	2
K	52	54	—2
1 (Hs) + .5K	53	52	1
2 (D)	53	56	—3
3 (Hy)	54	49	5 **
4 (Pd) + .4K	75	70	5 *
5 (Mf)	59	54	5 **
6 (Pa)	63	61	2
7 (Pt) + 1K	57	61	—4 **
8 (Sc) + 1K	63	60	3
9 (Ma) + .2K	61	59	2

* Signifies a difference reliable above the 5 per cent level of confidence.
** Signifies a difference reliable above the 1 per cent level of confidence.

her actions have placed her family in. Under the influence of this, the girl, on the one hand, may show excessive worry and anxiety and, on the other, deny to her own consciousness and others some of the severity of what has happened to her. It is of some interest that the broken home group of girls shows a distinctly more masculine score on scale 5. This might be related to an early development of aggressive self-reliance, which is probably more commonly forced upon the girls with broken homes than upon the others.

DISCUSSION

These studies have, in general, confirmed the findings of Capwell on girls and extended them to boys. The MMPI shows a significant differentiation of delinquent from nondelinquent boys and girls on several of the scales. The most definite differentiation occurs with scale 4 (Pd). As Capwell found, the delinquent girls are also differentiated on scale 6 (Pa) and, to a less certain degree, on several other scales.

Capwell drew her control groups from among school children of a

Minnesota town. She did not use the K correction. The mean scores for her nondelinquent control group of girls ran at nearly 50 throughout. If she had used K, there would have been a slight elevation of scales 7 and 8 since the average K of her control group was at a T of 53. In the present studies the nondelinquent girls, who were mostly from the larger urban center of Minneapolis and St. Paul, showed distinct elevations on scales 4, 6, 7, 8, and 9. Use of the K correction could not influence scales 6 and 9 and there is no certain explanation as to why the present samples of nondelinquent girls varied so much above the general norms.

The boys of the present samples who made up the nondelinquent control group also showed elevations on scales 4, 7, 8, and 9. In fact, in these studies the tendency for the control group to obtain high scores on these four scales obscures in part the discriminations from the delinquent samples. If one were to describe the trends indicated, one would say that the nondelinquent youths of the present studies were more asocial, sensitive, schizoid, and hyperactive than the general population and the girls were more so than the relatively similar samples of small-town girls used by Capwell. There was also a moderate tendency for the control group girls to be masculine in interest pattern as shown by scale 5. This was especially true of the higher socioeconomic sample from a private academy; by contrast the boys were more feminine than adult males in their interests as shown by scale 5.

Scales on which the delinquent boys and girls clearly exceeded the control means were scales 4, 6, 7, 8, and 9, which were the same scales that had a tendency to differentiate the control youths from the general population of adults used for standardization of the MMPI. The most significant findings were the high means for scale 4, indicating that among delinquents there are a large number having MMPI patterns like those of the clinically identified amoral, asocial psychopaths who were used in the derivation of the psychopathic deviate scale of the MMPI. This is, of course, consistent with expectations.

Delinquent girls more than boys have a tendency to be sensitive and feel that they are unduly controlled as indicated by scale 6. In some contrast, the delinquent girls lose some over-all defensive attitude in answering MMPI items and tend to get a K score that is nearer to the adult average than is true for the control girls. In contrast to this again, the delinquent boys obtain higher K scores and so would seem to have a more defensive test-taking attitude.

It is of interest that scales 1, 2, and 3 are not consistently elevated among delinquent boys or girls. This would indicate that neuroticism is not a characteristic of delinquents. The tendency toward a higher mean for scale 8 does indicate some schizoid elements present among delinquents.

It was possible to compare the amount of maladjustment, as indicated by MMPI scores, of metropolitan delinquent boys and non-metropolitan delinquent boys. This set of data indicated that the metropolitan boys were more maladjusted on the average. Notably, scales 1 and 3 showed a difference here indicating a greater neurotic factor among metropolitan cases. The hypothesis that rural judges are a little more prone to send a mildly maladjusted boy to a detention home or training school was indicated to have some foundation. These data support the value of developing more facilities for milder cases in rural areas.

It was also possible to compare the average scores of delinquent girls from broken homes with those of delinquent girls from unbroken homes. As has been found in other studies, the data here indicated the girls from broken homes to be more maladjusted. This was especially notable in scales 3 and 4, which represent hysterical tendencies, and the more frequent psychopathic syndrome present in all delinquent groups. The girls from broken homes were also a little more masculine in interests as measured by scale 5. Among the girls from unbroken homes there was a significantly higher K and a higher score 7. Interpretation of these data must be cautious though they suggest that the girls from unbroken homes are more defensive and possibly a little more likely to suffer from the neurotic factors giving rise to obsessive-compulsive behavior.

Personality Patterns of Juvenile Delinquents in an Area of Small Population

BY JAMES H. ASHBAUGH

THIS study was designed to check further the MMPI patterns of juvenile delinquents in contrast to nondelinquents. Previous data have indicated that there are significant differences in personality patterns between delinquents and nondelinquents, but these studies have been conducted in large cities or centers of large population. This work was intended to show whether the conclusions are applicable to areas of as small population as Benton County, Oregon. Benton County is located in western Oregon in the Willamette Valley. The county has a population of 31,524 (U.S. Census Bureau 1950). Corvallis, the largest city in the county and the fifth largest in the state, has 16,173 residents.

Two groups of 50 children each were selected for study. The first group was composed of juvenile delinquents from among the children referred to the juvenile court of Benton County over a period of two years. In selecting subjects for this group, an attempt was made to select "true" delinquents in the psychological sense rather than in the legal sense alone. For the purposes of this study a juvenile delinquent was considered as any child whose conduct deviates sufficiently from normal social usage to warrant his being considered a menace to himself, to his future life, or to society itself.

The second group was composed of nondelinquents and is referred to as the control group. This group was selected from the four high schools of the county: namely, Alsea, Corvallis, Philomath, and Monroe. In this selection there were some determining factors. Honor pupils and class leaders were omitted because delinquency is uncom-

EDITORS' NOTE. This study is from a thesis submitted in partial fulfillment of the requirements for the Ph.D. at Oregon State College. Mr. Ashbaugh is juvenile probation officer for Benton County, Oregon.

mon among them. The controls were matched or paired with the delinquents for sex, age, and residence in urban or rural areas. Any of either group achieving T scores of 70 or above on the L or F scales of the MMPI were eliminated from further consideration. The ratio of boys to girls in both groups was approximately three to one. This ratio was used because county, state, and national statistics indicate that the approximate ratio of the rate of referrals to the juvenile courts of boys to girls yearly is three to one.

Except for these factors, no other limitations were placed on acceptance of a subject. We feel that these two groups are fair samples for contrast of the delinquents and the nondelinquents in Benton County. In summary, there were 37 boys and 13 girls in each group; the two groups ranged in age from 13 to 18 with a median age of 15 years; and 20 per cent of each group lived in the rural area and 80 per cent in the urban area.

Test data for the study were gathered by the use of the following instruments: (1) the Henmon-Nelson Test of Mental Abilities; (2) the Minnesota Multiphasic Personality Inventory (Booklet Form); and (3) the Heston Personal Adjustment Inventory.

INTELLIGENCE TEST RESULTS

With the Henmon-Nelson Test, the mean IQ of the delinquent group was found to be 101.5 while that of the control group was 110.5. The critical ratio of the two groups was 3.43, which indicates a high reliability (see Table 1). The mean IQ of the delinquent group was 102.8 for the boys and 97.2 for the girls; for the control group it was 111.8 and 106.3 respectively. Only one case of the delinquent group was classified as a mental defective. The range of the delinquent group was 64 quotient points, while the range of the control group was 48.

TABLE 1. DISTRIBUTION OF IQ IN DELINQUENT AND CONTROL GROUPS

IQ	Delinquents[a]		Control Group[b]		Difference in Per Cent
	Number	Per Cent	Number	Per Cent	
140 and above	0	0	0	0	0
120–139	5	10	10	20	−10
110–119	12	24	17	34	−10
90–109	23	46	22	44	2
80–89	6	12	1	2	10
70–79	3	6	0	0	6
Below 70	1	2	0	0	2
Total	50	100	50	100	

[a] M = 101.5; SD = 15.08.
[b] M = 110.5; SD = 10.80. CR = −3.43.

MMPI FINDINGS

Validating statistics from the MMPI records are given in Table 2. In computing the statistics, mean raw scores were used instead of T scores. A reliable difference between the two groups is indicated in the L and F scores. The implications are that the delinquents were more likely to distort their scores in the favorable direction and also to be more careless or incapable in making discriminations on answers to the items. It should be kept in mind, however, that all records of more doubtful validity were rejected from the data so that the differences of Table 2 are attenuated toward validity.

The MMPI clinical scale statistics for the group are given in Table 3. The delinquents have a higher mean T score than the controls in all instances. A very reliable difference of mean T scores was found in six of the nine clinical scales. These were scales 3, 4, 6, 7, 8, and 9 (hysteria,

TABLE 2. MEAN RAW SCORES, STANDARD DEVIATIONS, AND CRITICAL RATIOS OF VALIDATING SCALES FROM THE MMPI

Scale	Delinquents, N = 50		Control Group, N = 50		Difference in Mean Score	Critical Ratio
	Mean Raw Score	SD	Mean Raw Score	SD		
L	5.00	2.57	3.48	1.64	1.52	3.62**
F	6.89	2.68	4.00	2.92	2.89	5.16**
K	13.86	5.38	13.84	4.70	0.02	0.02

** Signifies a difference reliable above the 1 per cent level of confidence.

TABLE 3. MEAN STANDARD SCORES, STANDARD DEVIATIONS, AND CRITICAL RATIOS OBTAINED FROM MMPI SCORES OF THE DELINQUENT AND CONTROL GROUPS

Scale	Delinquents, N = 50		Control Group, N = 50		Difference in Mean Score	Critical Ratio
	Mean T Score	SD	Mean T Score	SD		
1 (Hs)	57.7	14.12	51.8	11.04	5.9	2.20*
2 (D)	59.3	10.44	54.5	9.88	4.8	2.35*
3 (Hy)	57.5	10.08	52.7	7.32	4.8	2.75**
4 (Pd)	70.3	10.36	59.0	9.96	11.3	5.53**
5 (Mf)	55.3	10.53	53.2	12.06	2.1	0.96
6 (Pa)	63.3	4.83	52.8	4.71	10.5	11.41**
7 (Pt)	63.6	9.90	57.5	9.15	6.1	3.22**
8 (Sc)	64.0	10.00	57.2	11.44	6.8	3.15**
9 (Ma)	62.4	12.00	55.3	11.61	7.1	3.00**

* Signifies a difference reliable above the 5 per cent level of confidence.
** Signifies a difference reliable above the 1 per cent level of confidence.

TABLE 4. MEAN STANDARD SCORES, STANDARD DEVIATIONS, AND CRITICAL RATIOS
OBTAINED FROM THE MMPI SCORES OF THE BOYS IN THE DELINQUENT AND
CONTROL GROUPS

Scale	Delinquents, N = 37		Control Group, N = 37		Difference in Mean Score	Critical Ratio
	Mean T Score	SD	Mean T Score	SD		
1 (Hs)	58.1	16.53	52.0	9.79	6.1	1.89
2 (D)	58.4	11.09	55.5	9.38	2.9	1.17
3 (Hy)	57.2	10.09	53.1	7.60	4.1	1.98
4 (Pd)	69.7	10.50	60.2	9.77	9.5	3.97**
5 (Mf)	54.7	9.90	53.0	11.50	1.7	0.68
6 (Pa)	62.3	10.99	53.3	8.34	9.0	3.91**
7 (Pt)	63.9	9.44	59.4	7.99	4.5	2.17*
8 (Sc)	64.4	9.45	58.6	11.73	5.8	2.32*
9 (Ma)	62.2	10.13	56.0	9.55	6.2	2.14*

*Signifies a difference reliable above the 5 per cent level of confidence.
**Signifies a difference reliable above the 1 per cent level of confidence.

TABLE 5. MEAN STANDARD SCORES, STANDARD DEVIATIONS, AND CRITICAL RATIOS
OBTAINED FROM THE MMPI SCORES OF THE GIRLS IN THE DELINQUENT AND
CONTROL GROUPS

Scale	Delinquents, N = 13		Control Group, N = 13		Difference in Mean Score	Critical Ratio
	Mean T Score	SD	Mean T Score	SD		
1 (Hs)	54.5	9.67	50.4	12.91	4.1	1.21
2 (D)	61.0	8.49	52.5	8.96	8.5	2.38*
3 (Hy)	59.1	10.06	51.8	6.99	7.3	2.04
4 (Pd)	72.1	12.40	54.0	13.89	18.1	3.38**
5 (Mf)	57.8	12.89	54.5	6.29	3.3	0.82
6 (Pa)	64.7	10.68	50.5	12.06	14.2	3.04**
7 (Pt)	62.2	11.73	52.2	6.51	10.0	4.57**
8 (Sc)	62.9	10.73	54.7	11.20	8.2	1.82
9 (Ma)	64.8	13.03	53.0	14.99	11.8	2.05

*Signifies a difference reliable above the 5 per cent level of confidence.
**Signifies a difference reliable above the 1 per cent level of confidence.

psychopathic deviate, paranoia, psychasthenia, schizophrenia, and
hypomania). On scales 1 and 2 the critical ratios indicate a reliability
of the difference at better than the 5 per cent level.

Tables 4 and 5 further break down the clinical scale statistics presented in Table 3. These tables separate the boys from the girls and
give the clinical scale statistics for each of the groups. As in Table 3
the delinquents have a higher mean T score than the controls in all
instances. Between the groups of boys a very reliable difference of

mean T scores was found in two of the nine clinical scales. These were
4 and 6 (psychopathic deviate and paranoia). A very reliable difference of mean T scores was found in three of the nine clinical scales between the groups of girls. These were 4, 6, and 7 (psychopathic deviate,
paranoia, and psychasthenia). In scales 7, 8, and 9 the boys show a
difference reliable beyond the 5 per cent level. The delinquent girls
have a scale 2 difference reliable beyond the 5 per cent level and the
differences on scales 3 and 9 are very nearly as reliable.

Table 6 compares the occurrence of scale deviates at or beyond a
T score of 70 in the delinquent and the control groups. The most reliable difference is on scale 4 where 52 per cent of the delinquents made
T scores of 70 or above contrasted to only 12 per cent of the controls.

TABLE 6. PERCENTAGE OF SUBJECTS HAVING T SCORES EQUAL TO OR GREATER THAN
70 ON THE MMPI

Scale	Delinquent Abnormals		Control Abnormals		Difference in Per Cent	CR
	Number	Per Cent	Number	Per Cent		
1 (Hs)	9	18	3	6	12	1.87
2 (D)	6	12	2	4	8	1.40
3 (Hy)	7	14	1	2	12	2.26*
4 (Pd)	26	52	6	12	40	4.76**
5 (Mf)	5	10	1	2	8	1.70
6 (Pa)	10	20	2	4	16	2.54*
7 (Pt)	9	18	7	14	4	0.54
8 (Sc)	10	20	6	12	8	1.09
9 (Ma)	10	20	3	6	14	2.12*

*Signifies a difference reliable above the 5 per cent level of confidence.
**Signifies a difference reliable above the 1 per cent level of confidence.

HESTON INVENTORY

The Heston Inventory yields scores in six areas of adjustment:
analytical thinking, sociability, emotional stability, confidence, personal relations, and home satisfaction. The manual has separate norm
tables for girls and boys in which raw scores are converted into per-
centiles. For comparison of these two groups any individual whose percentile rating occurred below the 25th percentile was considered to
have a "poor" rating in that particular area of adjustment. A larger
percentage of the delinquents were rated by this criterion as having a
"poor" adjustment in all areas except sociability (see Table 7). In
three of the six scales, confidence, personal relations, and home satis-

TABLE 7. PERCENTAGE OF SUBJECTS IN DELINQUENT AND CONTROL GROUPS RANKING
BELOW THE 25TH PERCENTILE ON THE HESTON PERSONAL ADJUSTMENT INVENTORY

Scale	Delinquents		Controls		Difference in Per Cent	Critical Ratio
	No.	Per Cent	No.	Per Cent		
Analytical thinking ...	24	48	22	44	4	0.40
Sociability	15	30	15	30	0	0.00
Emotional stability ...	15	30	6	12	18	2.27*
Confidence	17	34	4	8	26	3.33**
Personal relations	19	38	5	10	28	3.47**
Home satisfaction	24	48	8	16	32	3.65**

* Signifies a difference reliable above the 5 per cent level of confidence.
** Signifies a difference reliable above the 1 per cent level of confidence.

faction, the differences between the two percentages are quite reliable.
In 1948, Cook (11) using the Heston Inventory also found significant
differences in the personality structure between delinquent boys and
nondelinquent boys. Comparing mean scores he found that the delinquents made lower scores, or were rated lower, on all scales.

DISCUSSION

The statutes of Oregon state that any child between the ages of 14
and 18 who violates any law of the state, or any city or village ordi-
nance, shall, when convicted in a court of law, be classified as a delinquent child. Just the fact that a boy or girl violates a law governing
speeding, smoking cigarettes, or general mischievousness may not make
him a delinquent in the psychological sense; but he would be considered a delinquent under the Oregon statutes. In selecting delinquents for the delinquent group, it was necessary to have knowledge
of the individual's background and to have observed and worked with
the individual in previous referrals. For the purpose of this study a
juvenile delinquent was considered on these criteria from the psychological viewpoint rather than the legal viewpoint. Thus we should expect more maladjustment and a higher rate of personality disorders
among such "true" delinquents than among normal children. The results as found in the MMPI and the Heston Inventory indicate that
conspicuous differences do exist between the two groups.

The MMPI shows the delinquent boys and girls were more generally unstable than the normal population. These differences particularly
indicate trends toward psychopathic and paranoid personality. These
are the persons who are emotionally shallow, lack ability to profit from
experience, are asocial, oversuspicious, oversensitive, and have delu-

sions of persecution. The greatest differences in the validating scales of the MMPI were in the L and F scales. The higher L was related to greater defensiveness among the delinquents. The higher F could be due to the greater amount of maladjustment in the delinquent group or more likely to a tendency to be careless in answering the items.

The greatest differences between the two groups on the Heston Inventory were in personal relations and home satisfaction. The author of the Heston Inventory believes that low scores on the personal relations scale are partially indicative of "paranoid" trends. This corresponds with the results found on the MMPI. Also, as was to be expected, a higher percentage of the delinquents expressed dissatisfaction with their home life.

It must be realized that some of the nondelinquents are maladjusted or have personality difficulties just as serious as those found among delinquents. Some of the nondelinquents too may need counseling and these findings are attenuated by this impurity of the control group.

The use of these two inventories is warranted in delinquency work and they are sufficiently discriminating. They are a good diagnostic tool. They are also probably useful as a prognostic tool in locating possible personality difficulties in order to do prevention work in delinquency.

MMPI Findings in the Rehabilitation
of Delinquent Girls

BY MARGARET LAUBER AND W. GRANT DAHLSTROM

THIS report is based upon studies of delinquent girls emphasizing their response to an institutional program. It also develops some differences among subgroups of girls in the institution. Findings are chiefly based upon MMPI profiles from thirty-five girls at Namequa Lodge, Illinois.

Namequa Lodge had been set up as an Association for the Care and Education of Problem Children through the Department of Child Welfare of the State of Illinois. The Federation of Women's Clubs of Rock Island County was the sponsor, and a large farm home was purchased as a residence. The Rock Island Board of Education established a fully accredited school under the direction of the Department of Special Education. All admissions to the Lodge were made through the Rock Island Juvenile Court. The superintendent of the East Moline State Hospital acted as chairman of the admission board which screened the girls for the rehabilitation program. Only fifteen girls were kept in residence at any one time.

After admission, each girl was fitted into the group activities with as little disturbance as possible. The work program was explained and her duties were assigned. She was enrolled in the school in whatever grade she had been attending, and she continued as far as possible the same courses she had previously been taking. Teaching was on a remedial plan which allowed considerable individual attention. As far as possible, the routine of the Lodge resembled a typical home of a large family. The staff participated in the activities informally, dining

EDITORS' NOTE. This is a modification of a Master of Arts thesis submitted to the Graduate College of the State University of Iowa by Mrs. Margaret Lauber. Mrs. Lauber is a psychologist in the Iowa Department of Public Instruction; Mr. Dahlstrom is a visiting assistant professor at the State University of Iowa.

with the girls, sharing the same living room, and accompanying them on numerous outings and parties. Considerable cooperation from nearby civic and church groups furnished contacts and social activities when the girls were ready for this freedom.

The whole plan of self-help was designed to offer an opportunity for the girls to gain responsibility, maturity, and self-understanding. When a girl seemed to have demonstrated her dependability, efforts were made to place her in as favorable a situation as possible for her further development. She was paroled to her own or a foster home or to a working home, with the full understanding that she could return to the Lodge if she was not satisfied. Those girls who could not fit into the routine of the Lodge were sent to other institutions in the state.

From among the forty-five girls cared for from January 1949 through 1950 at Namequa Lodge, thirty-five cases most available to the examiners were selected for intensive study. For the purposes of this study, the cases can be divided into two groups. Group I, the success group, is composed of those who made an adequate adjustment to the rehabilitation program and finally were placed on parole outside of the Lodge. This adjustment consisted of fitting into the routine of the Lodge and showing cooperation and a gradual increase in initiative and responsibility. These girls generally controlled their tempers, applied themselves to their studies, and gained increased self-understanding and social acceptability. They were finally paroled after an average residence of ten months and continued with adequate conduct in these homes, although a few of them returned to the Lodge voluntarily and sought more acceptable places.*

Group II, the failure group, consisted of a more diversified group of those who, for one reason or another, failed to make adequate adjustment to the program. Two girls ran away and were subsequently sent to the Geneva State Training School for Girls. Three girls showed marked emotional disturbances and were committed to a state hospital. The rest did not meet the standards of fitting into the routine of the Lodge or, when paroled, got into difficulty and were returned to Namequa for further work.

----

* These groupings were made in September 1950. The entry in Table 1 refers to the length of time outside of the Lodge up to that date (an average of approximately eight months). In September 1951, a re-examination was made of the status of the girls. Only three changes were clearly indicated. Cases 46921'8–' and 649823'71–' should have been placed in the failure group. Case 49682 37'–' should have been placed in the success group; her original placement in the failure group was made because she was still in the Lodge in September 1950. She subsequently met the standards for parole and has made excellent progress with this single trial.

A battery of tests was administered to the girls while in residence at the Lodge, including intelligence, educational achievement, interest, and personality tests. The booklet form of the MMPI was administered to each girl separately during her period of residency at the Lodge; most of these tests were given in the early months of 1950. A few cases were tested in other institutions after their failure in the program. Thus, in some cases, test results were obtained after some considerable work had been done with the girls. More than half of the group were retested with the MMPI, but since the cases were often specially selected to check on behavioral changes and since it was not a uniform procedure, little use will be made of this retest information.

Table 1 summarizes the pertinent background information. Several of the variables demonstrate the effects of the selection process leading

TABLE 1. BACKGROUND INFORMATION ON THE GIRLS IN THE PRESENT STUDY

	Success Group, N = 18		Failure Group, N = 17		Total, N = 35	
	Mean	SD	Mean	SD	Mean	SD
Age (in years)	16.4	0.7	16.3	0.8	16.4	0.7
Education (by grades) ...	10.0	1.2	8.8	1.6	9.4	1.6
Educational achievement score[a]	8.9	2.1	6.3	2.2	7.6	2.6
Intelligence[b]	102.6	12.6	92.9	11.3	97.9	12.8
Age of first known delinquency	12.0	2.1	11.4	2.1	11.7	2.2
Months in Lodge	10.2	7.4	12.8	8.4	11.5	8.1
Months out of Lodge	7.8	11.3				
Warner Index of Status Characteristics (medians)	69.5		73.0		72.0	

a Progressive Achievement Tests.
b Wechsler-Bellevue Intelligence Scale: Full Scale.

to the institution. The girls were between the ages of 12 and 16 when they were admitted. The mean age of this group at the time of the study was 16.4 years. They had resided in the Lodge an average of 11.5 months. Admittance requirements also stated that the girls were to be of at least average intelligence. When tested with the Wechsler-Bellevue Adult Intelligence Scale, they earned a mean full scale IQ of 98. In spite of this adequate intellectual capacity, the girls were educationally retarded both in terms of grade placement and measured scholastic achievement. They came from homes which were mainly (71.4 per cent) in the lower-lower classification of Warner's Index of

Status Characteristics (54). The remainder fell in the upper-lower (25.7 per cent) and lower-middle (2.9 per cent) classifications.

All the girls had been judged incorrigibly delinquent by the juvenile court after study of their cases. They were sent to Namequa Lodge for an indefinite period and were to be wards of the court until they reached legal age. Thirty-four were consistently truant; twelve had run away from home one to ten times. All rebelled at authority and were scornful of the law. Two sisters had been "lookouts" for a gang of boys who robbed cars and broke into stores and filling stations. Eight admitted to continual thieving and shoplifting, while thirty-two were known to have been involved in sexual delinquencies.

TABLE 2. T SCORE MEANS, STANDARD DEVIATIONS, AND DIFFERENCES BETWEEN THE SUCCESS AND FAILURE GROUPS OF DELINQUENT GIRLS

Scale	Success Group,[a] N = 18		Failure Group,[b] N = 17		Differences between Means
	Mean	SD	Mean	SD	
L	47.00	7.46	49.00	8.73	2.00
F	58.00	7.80	59.00	7.25	1.00
K	52.00	9.40	53.00	9.08	1.00
1 (Hs) + .5K	51.11	11.32	55.88	16.49	4.77
2 (D)	53.17	13.54	61.47	13.26	8.30
3 (Hy)	49.50	11.91	59.71	14.81	10.21 *
4 (Pd) + .4K	77.17	16.67	83.35	16.42	6.18
5 (Mf)	59.89	10.96	64.41	17.05	4.52
6 (Pa)	65.56	14.26	73.41	13.02	7.85
7 (Pt) + 1K	60.22	12.31	71.94	19.64	11.72 *
8 (Sc) + 1K	56.06	11.93	80.71	16.91	24.65 **
9 (Ma) + .2K	64.22	17.72	69.35	16.04	5.13

* Difference significant beyond the 5 per cent level of confidence.
** Difference significant beyond the 1 per cent level of confidence.
[a] Code of mean profile for success group: 4'6978–'.
[b] Code of mean profile for failure group: 4867'9231–'.

The results of the MMPI can be analyzed in two different ways. In Table 2 the means and standard deviations of the scores for each group are presented. It can be seen that the two groups show generally elevated scores on five of the nine clinical scales (Pd, Mf, Pa, Pt, and Ma). Both groups have particularly high mean values on the Pd scale. When these means are compared with means from nondelinquent groups as reported on adolescent girls by other workers, they differ from nondelinquents not so much in the particular scales which are high, but primarily in the much greater degree of deviation. The mean scores of the failure group show this relationship more clearly. When these means are coded, the sequence of high scores is similar to the results on delinquent girls reported by Capwell (5, also Study 1) and by Monachesi (42, 43, 44, also Study 2), but the code contains four primed values. In this important respect it differs greatly from test findings of normal adolescents, resembling more the codes of groups of known delinquents. Undoubtedly these high scores are a further result of the selective process leading to acceptance of the girls as treatment cases.

In general, the poor adjustment group had higher mean scores on each of the clinical scales, and statistically reliable differences were found on the Sc, Hy, and Pt scales. These findings are in full accord with the adverse behavioral items used to form the groupings of cases: problems of self-control, emotional stability, and self-insight. Even though these delinquents were segregated into a small isolated group and were given special attention and supervision, several girls in the failure group were so involved that other facilities were required. Two of these latter cases were ultimately given psychiatric diagnoses of psychosis. Nine others had psychotic episodes. In the good adjustment group, only one girl was considered of special psychiatric interest; the diagnosis was "psychoneurosis, hysteria."

A second way that the MMPI results may be treated is shown in the following List of Profile Codes, where the actual codes of each girl's test scores have been listed. The retest codes are also given when they are available. The validity scale values, shown after each profile code, meet the requirements set by Hathaway and Meehl very satisfactorily. The Cannot Say scores were negligible. We believe that these good validities can be attributed to the careful instructions and appeals for honesty and cooperativeness made in the individual testing sessions.

The scale 4 (Pd) values are prominent in all but two codes. This is the result that would be expected from the high mean values reported in Table 2. However, the large standard deviation for Pd in both groups suggested that the Pd score may not necessarily have been prominent in each test pattern. Therefore, the coded results clarify this feature very nicely. Similarly, although the results reported in Table 2 suggest that Sc is the main factor which differentiates the two groups in respect to their adjustment to the rehabilitation program, a clearer demonstration of the way that Sc and Pd operate in the individual cases is obtained from these lists. The most striking difference in the two columns is the lack of any 8 codes in the success group while nearly half of the codes in the failure group begin with 8. That is, although

List of Profile Codes

Success Group	Failure Group
'-329'68 (68) ;5,8,13	469'312-' (72) ;0,5,12
314'8792-' (47) ;4,3,13	4'69-1'27 (59) ;0,5,10
4'38791-' (47) ;7,10,19	483'29-' (47) ;4,3,15
'467-812'39 (57) ;0,3,17	48'73-1'2 (47) ;0,0,12
'4671-'2 (45) ;0,7,8	4839716'2-' (95) ;0,3,15
4'683-'2 (63) ;4,5,19	49682 37'-' (57) ;7,7,19
4'689-'2 (61) ;0,0,20	4968'723-'1 (57) ;0,10,9
'469-8'7 (51) ;5,8,17	4'98-2'13 (49) ;4,3,19
'469-328'71 (51) ;5,0,10	719326'48-' (53) ;5,5,12
469217'8-' (75) ;6,6,10	72'468-1'3 (76) ;4,12,12
46921'8-' (73) ;5,3,20	74698'2-1'3 (92) ;0,7,6
'46921-'7 (63) ;0,6,11	8'379-'2 (76) ;6,10,16
469'27-3'81 (37) ;4,8,12	84627'-'9 (76) ;7,3,20
479'-'83 (51) ;5,10,17	86247'-'93 (76) ;0,6,18
4'79-2'13 (51) ;5,8,17	846'792-' (41) ;4,5,8
'48-129'37 (72) ;4,3,12	8469'32-' (61) ;7,10,21
'48-2139'7 (72) ;4,3,12	84'63-7' (39) ;0,3,4
49'23-'17 (72) ;4,11,13	847'6-'139 (49) ;0,3,10
4'92-1'678 (70) ;0,7,12	84769'321-' (66) ;6,8,12
496'782-'13 (70) ;0,0,5	847'6392-' (61) ;6,5,9
94'678-32'1 (70) ;0,5,8	86497'13-'2 (51) ;0,9,10
647'8-231'9 (51) ;4,7,11	8746129'-' (72) ;4,7,21
'6748-'19 (57) ;0,7,10	8746'29 31-' (61) ;4,5,9
649823'71-' (55) ;4,3,13	982 6'47-' (84) ;5,8,11
4968'73-'1 (55) ;0,8,5	
742'81-' (57) ;7,8,21	
7'428-9'63 (59) ;0,3,12	
'96847-3'2 (68) ;0,5,6	
968'7413-' (66) ;0,11,21	
'9678-'123 (57) ;0,0,13	

there are certainly high Sc scores in the group with relatively good adjustment, in each instance the Pd or some other scale has an even higher value. In regard to these high Sc values, the failure group again differs markedly from the success group; the 8 is at a primed level in all but four codes of the failure group, but in only two of those of the success group.

While all the codes (including the retest codes) of the failure group are primed, one third of the codes from original tests of the success group do not have any score above 70. Perhaps it should be noted that the retests for both groups indicate a shift downward toward the lower T score values, the success group showing this to a greater extent. Among the particular scales, 2 (D) shows this shift most clearly, dropping appreciably, with a single exception, in every retest. In reference to these data the lack of complete coverage on the retesting program is to be lamented, for important biases may well exist among the available cases.

We feel that useful clinical indications can be gained from the consideration of the behavior of individual girls in close relation to the codes of their profiles. In the discussion following, we will refer to the various cases in the List of Profile Codes by citing the abbreviated codes of the first profile. If the reader wishes to add to his information the corresponding validity scores and, where one is available, the second profile code, these can be found in the List.

As may be expected, almost all the girls from both groups had some difficulty initially in getting along with the supervisors or with the other girls. These troubles included arguments and petty jealousies, crying spells and pouts, as well as rebellions against assignments or routines. A few cases (4'68̲3̲–'2, '467–81̲2̲'3̲9̲, and '–3̲2̲9̲'68) were exceptions to this pattern. They showed consistently angelic dispositions, willingness, and spontaneous cooperativeness which contrasted markedly with the remainder of the group. As can be seen, their codes lack the signs generally characteristic of the troublemakers and recidivists. In each case, these girls made easy and effective adjustments outside of the Lodge on a single trial.

Some girls demonstrated outstandingly serious and pervasive personality defects relatively early in their stay at the Lodge. Thus, cases having codes 8649̲7̲'13–'2, 846'792–', and 8469'32–' from the poor group were sent to East Moline State Hospital. The first two of these were diagnosed as suffering from some form of schizophrenia, the first having made a serious attempt at suicide. Cases with codes 719326'48–' and 31̲4̲'879̲2̲–' were also placed under psychiatric observation. The latter was diagnosed "psychoneurosis, hysteria," while the former was described as "personality disorder, undetermined type."

One interesting syndrome was observed relatively early in the period of residence in a surprisingly large group of girls. The behavior involved sudden screams and complaints of severe abdominal pain, usually appearing at night. This pattern of behavior was demonstrated by thirteen different girls at times rather separated from one another and in each instance subsequent blood counts for possible appendicitis were negative. Nine of these cases (4692̲1̲7̲'8–', 46921'8–', 496'782–'1̲3̲, 469'27–3'8̲1̲, 469'312–', 4968̲2̲ 37̲'–', 8649̲7̲'13–'2, 8469'32–', and 84769' 3̲2̲1̲–') had codes with scales 4, 6, and 9 primed. Only four ('4671–'2,

84627'–'9, 479'–'83, and 847'6–'1<u>39</u>) did not show all three elevations. Only three other cases in the study had this particular pattern in their codes, and each of these three had used some slightly different trick to obtain special attention.

Throughout their stay in the Lodge, the majority of the girls gradually settled down to their household duties and schoolwork. Only nine of the girls (84627'–'9, 74698'2–1'3, 864<u>97</u>'13–'2, 846'792–', 8469'32–', 48<u>39</u>716'2–', 483'29–', <u>72</u>'4<u>68</u>–1'3, and <u>982</u> <u>6</u>'47–') failed to qualify for at least one trial outside the Lodge. Some girls showed greater persistence in misbehavior or more extreme forms of misconduct. One of the problems which could be anticipated from the previous history of the group related to sexual activities. Ten cases were particularly troublesome in this respect, persisting in various forms of homoerotic and autoerotic practices despite efforts to modify their behavior. Their codes are 46921'8–', <u>649823</u>'71–', 496'782–'<u>13</u>, '48–129'37, 8746129'–', 469'312–', 74698'2–1'3, 8469'32–', 48<u>39</u>716'2–', and <u>72</u>'4<u>68</u>–1'3. The codes from these cases show the common factors of 48 or 84, several of which are at a primed level.

Similarly, various forms of aggression were consistent problems from a few cases with these profiles: 719326'48–', 496'782–'<u>13</u>, 49<u>682</u> <u>37</u>'–', and 48<u>39</u>716'2–'. All had frequent episodes of direct physical assault on other girls and each case had a 9 score at a primed level in her code. Two other girls ('48–129'37 and 8746129'–') frequently broke things in their temper tantrums but had no instances of assault. One of these lacks the 9 elevation in her MMPI code.

One further set of observations should be collated with the results in the List of Profile Codes. The good adjustment group, partly by definition, showed fairly consistent and effective application to the educational program, but the poor group showed a variety of responses to this work. Four cases (469'312–', 49<u>682</u> <u>37</u>'–', 4'98–2'13, and <u>982</u> <u>6</u>'47–') resembled the good group in working hard and achieving well in their studies; each of these had codes of either 49 or 9. A larger group having profiles of 84627'–'9, 8746129'–', 847'6–'1<u>39</u>, 8'<u>379</u>–'2, 864<u>97</u>'13–'2, 846'792–', 8469'32–', and 84769'<u>321</u>–' showed extremely poor attention to the lectures and lessons, were distractible and unconcerned about failure. Each of these girls had high 8 scores and the behavior seemed to correspond to this withdrawal and disturbance of mentation.

Two cases (48<u>39</u>716'2–' and 483'29–') showed a marked and persistent dislike for schoolwork and their similar 48' codes suggest a degree of similarity to the previous group. Three cases differed from the previous reactions in being quite markedly concerned about success or failure and about getting assignments finished on time. They each reacted quite emotionally to tests, and their tension and nervousness seemed to interfere with their efficiency. Their profiles are 719326'48–', 74698'2–1'3, and 72'468–1'3. All three of these girls had scale 7 as the prominent feature of their codes.

Extensive generalizations are not warranted from data obtained relatively late on a small group of girls already well along on a special rehabilitation program. The material cannot be offered as a reliable basis for predicting severe delinquency or even for anticipating the outcome of therapeutic efforts since the study was not rigidly designed. The results do seem to be internally consistent and to agree with what we feel is fairly general clinical practice. The material also shows that the MMPI in its present form provides some objective basis for describing and quantifying two important areas in the adjustment problems of delinquents. First, the findings show that the girls are relatively homogeneous, the psychopathic, paranoid, and hypomanic trends being the salient characteristics. Secondly, they reflect features which differentiate various subgroups among these delinquent individuals. In our study, the girls who profited least from the program generally had more severe emotional problems and the Inventory profiles reflected these trends. Also, the girls reacted in a variety of ways to the special measures instituted, and the test results again seem to have been in accord with these variations: aggressions, sexual deviations, or educational and motivational problems. Further study aimed at clarifying and confirming these findings is clearly indicated.

study 5

The Relationship between MMPI Profiles and
Later Careers of Juvenile Delinquent Girls

BY STARKE R. HATHAWAY, DONALD W. HASTINGS,

DORA F. CAPWELL, AND DOROTHY M. BELL

SINCE the Capwell profiles and records were still accessible in 1951 when funds became available for additional study of delinquency, it was possible to extend her findings by a longitudinal follow-up to test whether the profiles of the public and reform school girls might relate to their later careers. This follow-up was especially desirable because newer methods of statistical treatment have made possible some evaluation of whole profiles in contrast to the single variable analysis which was used in the earlier studies.

We accordingly sent a social worker into the field to discover what she could about the later careers of both the public and detention school girls. This project was begun almost exactly seven years after the initial tests by Capwell. By the time of the follow-up, the delinquent girls had reached a median age of 23 and the public school group a median age of 22 years. All the public institution registeries in Minnesota were checked for both groups of names, and an effort was made to find every girl. Where possible, the girl was interviewed by the field worker. When she could not be directly interviewed, as much information as possible was gathered from relatives and others who knew about her.

Of the 102 girls in the original public school sample, some general information was obtained regarding 73; but adequate and reliable data were obtained for only 28. Of the 110 delinquent girls, reliable data were obtained for 92; and adequate information was found for 50. Most of those not found had left no traces to be followed with reasonable effort or had moved to another state.

EDITORS' NOTE. Dr. Hastings is head of the Department of Psychiatry and Neurology, University of Minnesota; Miss Bell is a junior scientist, University of Minnesota.

Fifty-five per cent of the 73 public school girls were married at the time of the follow-up, contrasting with 84 per cent of the 92 delinquent girls. One illegitimate child was on record among the public school girls, fifteen illegitimate children among the delinquent girls. These fifteen did not include the illegitimate children with which many of the girls were pregnant at the time of original admission to the reform school.

The investigating social worker and two other judges familiar with social history data, after reading the information from all the follow-ups, selected those histories that were reliably complete and divided them into two subgroups. The first subgroup, composed of seventeen delinquent and two public school girls, consisted of those judged to have made a poor subsequent adjustment. It should be kept clearly in mind that this judgment was based upon hospitalization for mental disorders or other evidences of social deficiency. *Personality or social factors not involving obvious social dependency were not emphasized.* Even though a girl was personally odd or unconventional, she was accepted in this follow-up as having made a good adjustment when her record included no reason for social action such as placement of illegitimate children, workhouse sentence, or other institutionally treated misbehavior or mental illness. If a girl showed these classes of behavior but was kept in the family group, which substituted in a sense for public institutions, she was considered similar to those who actually did require public attention.

In contrast to girls with later social dependency, as thus defined, the second subgroup consisted of twenty-six public school and thirty-three detention school girls whose subsequent histories indicated fair to good social self-support. The final differentiations between poor and good were based on independent agreement of two of the three judges and final agreement of all three after discussion. Cases on which there was insufficient information were not classified.

Capwell administered the MMPI twice to all the girls in her study. The first profiles from delinquents were obtained near the time of admission of the girl to the home school, and the second tests were given six to fifteen months later. In the analyses of this paper, both profiles from a girl are used if both are valid. If only one is valid, then that one is used as the exemplary one.

Preparatory to accepting MMPI profiles for analysis, all those in which there was a ? T score of 70 or greater were eliminated. Among the remainder accepted for analysis, 18 per cent of the public school profiles had a ? T score in the range of 60 to 69 inclusive, and 10 per cent of those from delinquent girls had ? scores in this T score range.

Nearly all records having a T score of 80 or more on F were automatically eliminated. Of the public school group, four girls had F scores greater than 60; but these four were clearly valid, since several of the other clinical scales were at or below the mean. The highest one of these four F scores was T score 70. As might be expected, more delinquent girls obtained high F scores. Ten of the records considered acceptable showed F scores between 70 and 79 inclusive. One F score of 80 (raw score 16) was retained in the analysis because several of the clinical scores were low, an unlikely occurrence if the girl had answered invalidly through carelessness.

No limits were placed upon the values of L and K among profiles acceptable for this study. Three of the public school records showed L's of 70 or more. The raw scores for these three were 11, 10, and 10. Among the delinquent girls there was surprisingly little difficulty with high L. Of the records retained with L scores of 70+, the largest showed a raw score 15; there was one 13, one 12, one 11, and three 10's. Most of these high L cases will be specifically singled out in the analysis below.

The reader should be aware that all the data of this paper are based upon profiles in which the scores have been K corrected. Capwell did not use the K correction because it was not available at the time. Later scoring of her records showed that the mean K score of her delinquent girls was at about the adult value. The mean for the public school girls was higher than the adult mean. The use of the K correction decreases the observed over-all differentiation of delinquent from non-delinquent girls. This loss of group differential power does not mean that the K corrected scores lose *individual* validity. Until definitive evidence is available, we assume that the K corrections are valid.

After culling unacceptable cases and profiles, there remained as a basis for the analyses 55 profiles from 28 public school girls and 94 profiles from 50 delinquent girls. Of the 28 public school girls, 2 were considered to have made poor later adjustment and 26 good. Among the 50 delinquent girls, there were 33 good and 17 bad adjustments on the basis of the histories. It should be kept in mind that the following analyses treat with two profiles from most of the girls. Usually no distinction is made between the two profiles when the reference is to good or bad signs which could, therefore, be on either one. It may be that the first profile from a girl will indicate a good adjustment; the second, a bad adjustment. Usually we indicate such discrepancies in the discussion.

To simplify the profile analysis of MMPI information in relation to the follow-ups, we will treat only with code patterns and, for the most part, only with the two highest coded scores (35, 57, 58).

CODE PATTERNS

As a first step, all profiles used in the analysis were classified according to the first two code numbers of the profile. Two graphs (like those in the *Atlas* (37)) were made showing the relative frequencies of each combination and permutation of the first two code numbers. When these classified frequency patterns from the subgroups were compared, a number of clear contrasts appeared. Some of these contrasts seemed useful and reliable, but the data were too complex to present in a short report and frequencies for classes were small. Accordingly, most of the rarer code types were disregarded; and the classes were condensed into five subgroups of patterns where the useful information seemed to be concentrated. These subgroupings will be discussed successively as the more important findings in this report. Since the groupings were made up after the data had been graphed, they were not random in occurrence and unfortunately not legitimate for statistical analysis to estimate the reliabilities of the differences. As an example to show the order of differences discussed here, one chi square is given below in the data on the code types 4–, 49, and 94.

Code Type –

The first grouping is made up of all those profiles the codes of which showed no high points (codes beginning with –). Twenty-seven per cent of the fifty-five valid public school codes showed no codable high point. At least one of these normal-looking profiles was obtained by eleven of the twenty-eight girls in the adequate follow-up group of public school girls. Two of the eleven had codes with no high point on both the first and second tests. For the nine girls where only one of the two profiles was without a codable high point, the first MMPI was the one showing the lower values; none of the second profiles was at all abnormal in form or elevation. Actually, no single profile point from the eleven girls exceeded a T score of 70 on any scale.

One of these eleven public school girls who had at least one no-high-point profile was rated as having made a poor adjustment. This girl had for her first MMPI a code of –769 138;6,2,14. Her second code was

'4–679;4,4,19. The latter code was a worse type and is discussed in a later section. This girl was a moderate social responsibility. She had become a wanderer, moving from one town to another, working briefly in each. Shortly after the MMPI's were administered (she was only 12 at the time of the first testing), she married and had one legitimate child whom she never hesitated to leave in order to wander about the country. She seemed to have few close friends and went about with men older than herself. At the time of the follow-up she was 19. The family background was adverse; a sister had two illegitimate children by the time this girl was in the eighth grade. It would appear from the social data that the two MMPI's may have been given at a time of transition between the earlier fairly good adjustment and the later irresponsibility.

From among the fifty delinquent girls, where there were adequate data for rating, only two profiles were obtained that had no codable high point. These were both from one girl. This girl's IQ fell in the dull-normal range. Apparently she made a good marriage to an older man and went to live on a farm, in which protected environment she did very well. No other of the ninety-four profiles from the fifty delinquent girls was without codable high points.

In summary, the girls having one or both profiles with no codable high points in the two tests were mostly public school girls. Only one of the eleven public school girls with these low profiles was rated as having a bad subsequent history. She obtained an adverse 4– type profile on her second testing. The one girl among the delinquents who obtained such profiles adjusted well in spite of the handicap of low intelligence. The probability appears fair, therefore, that a girl who has no codable high points in her MMPI profile is a good risk for making a satisfactory social adjustment.

1, 2, 3, and 7

The next grouping includes all codes having 1, 2, 3, or 7 as the first coded high scale. In usual clinical interpretation, these profiles would include those considered as neurotic in form rather than behavior problem or psychotic. Twenty-nine per cent of the public school girls (eight girls) obtained among them ten codes having one of the neurotic scales as a first or highest point. With most of these ten codes, the associated second test was not greatly unlike a neurotic type or was a normal-appearing profile. One of the girls showed a shift from a '4786–913;5,3,13 in the first test to a more neurotic 7'428 63–9;5,6,14 in the second. All eight of the girls adjusted uneventfully.

Only three among the delinquent group obtained a neurotic profile. The first of these had Hs as the highest point on both administrations. In spite of a difficult home situation, she adjusted very well. Her two codes were 13482'76–X;12,11,26 and 1483'96–;5,9,21. The first was invalidated by the L and the second was not a pure neurotic type, nor, for that matter, was it a behavior disorder type of code. The K was high in both codes. This was a Negro girl who was sent to the detention home chiefly because of a "childlike" type of delinquency that ultimately led to an illegitimate pregnancy. Her father was in a state hospital for the insane and her mother was dead. At the time of the follow-up she was 23 years old, a good worker, and considered determined and likely to continue her good adjustment.

The second of the three girls had a mildly neurotic type first code ('23467 81–;6,5,18) and a second code (4'732 896–;5,3,19) which still showed neurotic features. At the time of the follow-up she was 25 and apparently adjusting very well. She had an average IQ and made a successful marriage after leaving the detention school. Even though the 4 is high on the second code, 7, 3, and 2 are also elevated so that the profile has clearly neurotic features.

The third of these girls was the only one having neurotic codes who made what was judged to be a poor subsequent adjustment. The first MMPI from this girl was invalid because of a high ? score. The mildly neurotic type code of her second test was '2478–93;7,3,15. The L of 7 is quite high. At the time of the follow-up, the girl, who was of Mexican-American parentage, was considered very undependable. She frequently became drunk and took no responsibility for the illegitimate child that had been the reason for her commitment. Her IQ at various times ranged between 62 and 79. It is interesting that the staff at the hospital where her child was delivered considered her "responsible, calm, neat, and ambitious." In this case, one might emphasize the special handicaps in conjunction with few compensating assets.

In summary, codes obtained from 29 per cent of the public school girls fell into this mildly neurotic classification; contrasting with this, 6 per cent of the delinquent girls had such codes. Only one of the eleven girls from the combined groups was rated as bad, and her history was somewhat equivocally so. Apparently, if girls with neurotic codes are fortunate enough to marry well or otherwise get into a fairly good environment, few, if any, will continue in delinquent social maladjustment. To extend further the implications of the evidence, girls who obtain a neurotic pattern profile appear less probable to get into trouble in the first place, since these codes are relatively rare among the delinquent girls.

Code combinations with one of these four neurotic variables as a second highest point were rare and scattered with the minor exception of 47 codes. Six per cent of delinquent good outcome codes and 9 per cent of delinquent poor outcome codes were of this type. Apparently the 7, although an influence toward better outcome, is not enough to balance the more powerful unfavorable trend associated with variable 4.

4–, 49, and 94

Among the fifty-five public school profiles, only one from each of three girls was in one of these categories. These three codes were all of the '4– type and thus did not represent very severe patterns, since the whole profile of each was below a T of 70. Two of the three girls did well according to the follow-up. The third girl had as her two profiles '–769 138;6,2,14 and '4–679;4,4,19. She was discussed above with the no-high-point group. It is interesting in the present context to note again that she was the only one of the girls in that group who appeared to be a continuing delinquent.

Of the ninety-four profiles obtained from the delinquent girls, eighteen were in one of these classes. These eighteen profiles were obtained from fifteen girls. This constituted about 30 per cent of the delinquent girls, a much higher proportion than occurred among the public school girls. The difference was particularly marked since about half of the profiles were elevated at their highest point to 70 or more T score. There was a tendency for the other profile for most girls to be of a different class, although usually 4 remained a high point. The most common variant was a pattern beginning with 6. In the follow-up study of the fifteen girls, eight were judged to have made an exceptionally poor adjustment although among them were several whose profiles were only moderately elevated. For example, one girl obtained these two profiles: '4–31 67;3,1,8 and '4–6713;1,4,7. It is notable that both have a low K. Although neither of these profiles was very high, the girl made an exceedingly poor adaptation and at the time of the follow-up was in jail pending investigation for stealing checks from the United States mail.

There was only one girl among these eight whose second profile had a scale other than 4 as its highest point. This girl obtained the profiles '4–9X;10,2,20 and '648–9;5,4,20. In this case the K is higher. After leaving the detention school, she was married and had one child. Her husband was an alcoholic and forced her to work. She frequently left her home and went to stay with her parents, and she was rated as irresponsible and impulsive. It is interesting that although she was given a poor rating in the follow-up, the above constituted the only definite complaint about her. Unlike the other seven cases, she had not been in any major difficulty. Her history is again referred to among the 6 type profiles below.

One of the seven more severe cases was an American Indian girl with the profile codes 4'9687–;1,14,4 and 94'8726–;4,11,4. The K in this case is unusually low. Twenty-two at the time of the follow-up, she had an IQ in the superior range although it varied greatly over several testings. She was originally committed for grand larceny. This girl was reputedly homosexual. However, her chief area of maladjustment lay in personal relationships, where she was unreliable, arrogant, and disdainful of any conventions.

Another of the cases making poor adjustment showed these two profiles: 4'98 76–1X;4,16,14 and 41'836297–;6,2,18. Of low IQ (about 70), she was rated as unstable and unreliable in work and social relationships. She was a white girl married to a Negro. About the time of the follow-up, when she was 23, she made an attempt at suicide after a quarrel with her husband. She is also mentioned below with reference to the 8 type.

Another illustrative case among these 8 girls had profiles '496–21; 5,2,12 and '4–9287;3,2,12. Neither of these profiles was particularly elevated, but both were clearly among the poor prognostic types. This attractive-appearing girl was committed for drunkenness, late hours with men, and threatening to kill her mother. An unusual amount of effort was expended trying to help her. She was studied by a psychiatric team that made recommendations; her mother cooperated even to the extent of moving to another town. On the second evening spent in the new town, she was out nearly all night at a night club and in the company of several boys known as town behavior problems. Our last information was that she had deserted her child and husband and gone to another state.

One of the worst among these girls had the profiles 4'9687–;3,4,11 and 94'68–2;3,5,13. She was 22 years old at the time of the follow-up. Her intelligence was superior adult. She had originally been committed because of sexual promiscuity, stealing, and other offenses. Her career continued in like pattern during stormy paroles and after release. White, she married a 53-year-old Negro after having three illegitimate children. These children all had Negro fathers. The girl was in a mental hospital for three months after repeated parole infractions.

The eight girls with socially dependent histories constituted 47 per cent of all observed bad-outcome girls among the delinquent follow-up cases. They produced seven of the fifteen known illegitimate children of the follow-up period. A common characteristic was that they showed, with the slight exception of the first girl described above, unequivocally poor adjustment.

No one of the seven delinquent girls with these profile types who had a good later record obtained adverse profile patterns on both testings. Only three of the seven had 4 among other high points on both testings. The one with the most adverse appearing patterns obtained profiles '4698–;0,7,13 and 49'867–1;2,5,10. This girl, 21 at the time of the follow-up, was still unmarried and a steady worker although her home background was somewhat adverse. She was rated conscientious and ambitious. Several of the seven barely managed to adjust and had they been among the public school group would certainly have been considered bad. For example, one girl had codes '69–2;2,2,15 and '94–21;4,3,16, neither code being very severe. She had been committed because of sexual promiscuity, lying, and stealing. Her intelligence was average. She completed only the eleventh grade at the detention home and was an underachiever. She made a good marriage to a steady man and seemed to be acceptably good within the definition of this study.

In summary, the three classifications 4–, 49, and 94 were associated with a high probability of bad outcome. This was particularly true when repeated testing showed the same pattern and when 4 was a high point with no strong neurotic tendency evidenced by elevation of scales 1, 2, 3, and 7. The adverse indication was still fairly strong even when scale 4 was not so high as T score 70 but was clearly a peak in the profile. Although the statistic may not be entirely legitimately used, a chi square was applied as exemplary of the order of differences being discussed. The fourfold table had the entries of eight bad histories and seven good histories among girls with one of these profile types and nine bad and twenty-six good histories for girls without such a pattern. The resultant chi square is 3.6 which is at about the 5 per cent confidence point. It is unfortunate that the numbers are so small in these subgroups, or rather that there are no statistics to handle the interrelated data of the several overlapping groups where partial cross validations may be found in the consistency of the various trends, themselves too weak to be creditable.

6–, 86, 96, and 46

The patterns formed with scale 6 are apparently relatively favorable indications, although they are a common type among delinquent girls. Among fifty-five public school profiles, only four were classifiable among these categories. All four of the girls who had such a pattern made a good adjustment according to the follow-up.

Twenty-four of the ninety-four delinquent profiles had 6 as a prominent high point. These twenty-four profiles came from twenty of the fifty girls, making up 46 per cent of the whole group. Only three of the twenty girls were among the total of seventeen classified as having made a poor adjustment subsequently. One of the three with a poor outcome had codes '643–;2,2,17 and 4'368179–;3,2,23. This girl, who was 24 at the time of the follow-up, was a white girl married to a Negro. She was described as a "smooth, tricky girl, antagonistic toward authority." The husband reputedly ran a house of prostitution, and the girl seemed chiefly characterized by what appeared to be a need to defy convention. It is noteworthy that her second profile shows a more adverse pattern.

A second of these three girls had codes '4–9X;10,2,20 and '648–9; 5,4,20. This girl was one of those described under 4– in the last section above although she had a 6 type profile for her second test. She made a poor adjustment, showing marked and apparently calculated defiance of convention.

The third girl had codes 6847'92–3;3,11,15 and 6'748–3;5,6,15. Her IQ was about 75 and she was 22 at the time of the follow-up. The only facts explaining the poor rating given her were that she had married a Negro and was said to have been in a workhouse (a point that was never verified).

A high scale 6 was a dominant score in both codes of most of the seventeen girls who made a good adjustment. Often one of the neurotic scales would also be elevated although no profile occurred with the combination of 6 and a neurotic score as the first two numbers of the code.

Codes with 64 or 46, where the adverse variable 4 is elevated with the 6, occurred only twice among the public school girls but were more frequent with delinquent girls. These constituted 23 per cent of the good profiles and 19 per cent of the bad. Here again, although the frequency of such profiles is certainly not reliably greater among the profiles of good outcome cases, there appears to be a distinctly inhibiting influence upon the adverse influence of variable 4 when variable 6 is also high enough to be coded. The trend seems the more sure since the number of bad profiles among the 46's was three times that among the 64's. A public school girl, with the rather elevated profiles 48'96173–;4,7,10 and 469'7 823–;4,12,13, provides an interesting example. At the time of her original study, Capwell found this girl to be nearly as delinquent as the committed girls. By the time of the follow-up, however, she had made a good marriage, had settled down, and was obviously a good outcome. Her sister said fervently, "She sure changed and the family never expected it."

An interesting, although tentative indication, comes from the combination where the profile high point is 4 and the low point is 6. This high-low combination occurred with only two delinquent girls, and the adjustments of both were rated bad. The combination also occurred with only two public school girls, and these were the two whose adjustments were rated bad. We have felt, from clinical experience, that a low scale 6 is often an adverse indication from a hospitalized patient whose profile does not have high points to indicate his illness. We have suspected that such cases are likely to be controlled paranoid types who falsify answers to hide their paranoid thoughts. The present data would seem consistent with this.

In summary, the evidence indicated that scale 6, when elevated even in the company of scale 4, represents a relatively good sign for satisfactory behavior. It seems possible that the ability of a delinquent girl to feel paranoid resentments is a positive factor in helping her toward later adjustments.

8

Variable 8 was a common point among the top two scales for all the girls. Twenty-six per cent of the public school profiles and 30 per cent of those from delinquent girls had a high 8. No public school girl with an 8 scale high had obvious difficulty in adjustment. Codes with an 8 made up only 11 per cent of those profiles from girls with bad outcomes, but they included 35 per cent of the codes from good-outcome girls. Seven different bad-outcome girls supplied the seven 8 type codes. On the whole, these particular girls were somewhat milder bad cases; and when they had really bad outcomes, they tended to obtain a pattern with a high scale 4 as the second of the two codes.

Perhaps appropriately to the schizoid character of the 8 variable, both the girls who attempted suicide and were briefly in a mental hospital for behavior considered possibly psychotic had 8 as a prominent code character. The first was described above among the 4's. She had codes 4'98 76–1X;4,16,14 and 41'836297–;6,2,18. The other girl had codes 4'6897–2;6,10,19 and '46–31;11,8,13. She dived off a bridge in an exhibitionistic attempt at suicide. After eight days in a state hospital she was released. Although she was not considered psychotic, she was impulsive and intellectually dull. The third girl of the seven had a first code 4'87–312;3,8,13 and a second '49–631;2,6,13. Included among the 4's above, she was not specifically described there. Although this girl bore an illegitimate child, she was considered honest and a hard worker.

Another girl, an Indian, had codes 468'97–;2,10,5 and 986'47–3;3,0,66. This girl was rated responsible and logical, "a timid, withdrawn girl." Her adjustment was considered bad because she was sexually promiscuous and had three illegitimate children. Still another bad-outcome girl was described among the 6's, where she can be identified by the first code 6847'92–3.

Since nearly all these cases had 8 as one of several underlined high points (and thus equal in value to at least one other score), none of the case histories should be weighted heavily as typical of high 8 profiles. The only girl who showed a definitely high 8 profile had codes '8764–1;4,4,17 and 84'32716–X;15,10,28. The second code is notable for the 15 L score and 28 K. The girl had an illegitimate child and was noted as "rebellious and stubborn."

In summary, there is at least a hint that the schizoid variable 8 is an indication of fair adjustment as here considered. Among the few with high 8 type profiles, there were no clearly psychotic girls, but the only two among the whole group who spent time in a psychopathic hospital under suspicion of psychosis had profiles where 8 was one of the higher points. There did seem to be a tendency for these girls to be rebellious and withdrawn. Again, as with the 6 variable, the 8 may partly cancel the adverse indication of the 4 variable.

GENERAL PREDICTION

Considered as a practical study, the most interesting question about these relationships between test results and later careers concerns the degree to which the later career could have been predicted from inspection of the test patterns. In order to throw some light on this question, we submitted the profiles obtained by the 50 home school girls to five persons moderately skilled in the interpretation of MMPI data. These persons were uncontaminated with any knowledge of the specific findings of the study but, of course, knew that the scales Ma and Pd were frequently associated with repeated infractions of the law and related difficulties. The five clinicians were told that among these 50 girls, 17 had continued to be social problems. The task presented was that the profiles should be separated into two groups of 33 and 17, representing the rater's best guess as to the outcome.

Under these conditions three of the five raters missed 8 and two missed 9 cases among the 33 good predictions. Since a miss in prediction of good outcome also forced a miss in the prediction of bad outcome, the total misses among 50 were twice these numbers; the raters were 64 to 68 per cent right. The most likely percentage right expected from random guessing would be 55.2 per cent. When the five raters were combined so that three of five votes determined the prediction, the percentage right was 70. The chi square test of the significance of this distribution indicated a reliability at better than the 3 per cent probability level.

From these findings we feel encouraged to consider the MMPI profiles as usefully related to outcomes, and it is reasonable to expect that further knowledge of the instrument would permit still better accuracy of prediction. It is of some interest to note that 6 of the 8 or 9 persons misplaced were universally misplaced by all five raters. At the moment no explanation for the discrepant outcomes can be discovered, and there is no obvious hint in the profiles that could be used for better sorting in the future.

DISCUSSION

Obviously the outcome of parole and discharge from a correctional institution is a complicated function of the personality of the girl involved and of the environment into which she is discharged. It would be unlikely that any psychometric or other procedure could achieve a perfect prediction of subsequent outcome in the adjustment of the juvenile delinquent girls. The most we may expect to do is discover signs that the girl merits particular attention and help, being a probably good prospect for benefit from such personal help and environmental supervision as we may give her. It is rather easy to demonstrate differences between girls already delinquent and those not so; to start with the delinquent group and make a prediction about the future is the more difficult problem. Most of the pertinent literature deals with the outcome during parole. This alone is difficult, but in this study we have been concerned chiefly with the adjustment in the period after parole.

The social factors determining adjustment after leaving reform school and parole seemed often to be beyond a girl's control, but this was by no means always true. A girl who is aberrant in physical type or of low intellect has a social adjustment handicap that is not a product of her personality. By contrast, a girl who marries a drunkard or returns to an adverse family setting could be considered to have contributed to the situation in ways we could relate to her personality. Thinking in this line, we might expect to predict bad marriages by personality test, yet in an individual case it often seems that the girl could not have married otherwise from lack of opportunity to marry anyone else or from the inaccessibility to her of data that might warn her.

It should be clear, a priori and from these data, that no single MMPI profile, however adverse or good in its apparent characteristics or probability class, can comfortably be accepted as a sole determinant of our action and expectation about a given girl. Some of the girls with unfavorable profiles made good adjustment, although more did not than did so. Some of those girls having apparently good prospects for adjustment failed to live up to the promise, although more of them came out well than otherwise. The stability of the husbands seemed an important determinant in the future of the delinquent girls. At any rate, within the present data, delinquent girls seemingly headed for more trouble in several instances reversed the trend and made very good adjustments after marrying a steady, often older, man.

It is unfortunate that the numbers in the subgroups are so small as to leave the findings unsatisfactory in reliability. We consider it to be probable that the majority of the observed trends will hold with future clinical experience. The data are presented here with the hope that the clinician may have, in the meantime, a degree of validity for the judgments and predictions that must be made while we await the more adequate studies.

Although the two profiles from a given girl were often different because of changes in the girl or other unidentified factors, a fair amount of relationship between the profile types and later careers of the girls existed. This relationship chiefly depended upon interpretation of variables that our experience in other clinical settings led us to expect would apply. Specifically, MMPI variables coded 4 and 9 were the best indicators of continuing delinquency. In a general way, the neurotic variables 1, 2, 3, and 7 and even the more psychotic variables 6 and 8 were indications of good outcomes as here evaluated. All these relationships depended upon the dominance of the given variable in coded profiles.

We hesitate to state broad principles in more than a very tentative way, but at least one seems warranted. MMPI variables 4 and 9 were originally derived from patients characterized by extrovertive and generally social interaction activities. *Social* is not meant to convey necessarily good behavior but rather behavior that involves a society, someone to steal from, react against, influence, and the like. All the other variables considered here turn more inward; neurotic preoccupation, schizoid preoccupation, even paranoid sensitivity, have this personal trend. It is our tentative hypothesis that the development or preservation in a girl of a capacity for intrapersonal sensitivities as a reaction to interpersonal contacts is a good sign relative to cultural conformity; and the favorable import of scales 1, 2, 3, 7, and 8 is related to that intrapersonal aspect.

This is true even though the intrapersonal sensitivity factor is often, in other ways, maladaptive; it is true even if the trend is paranoid so that the girl complains that she is watched or controlled too much; it is just when these intrapersonal reactions do not trouble her that she is a bad risk. The emphasis should be placed upon the fact that she is sensitive to others. This is consistent with earlier work on the psychopathic deviate variety of psychopathic personality where stress was placed upon the absence of neurotic symptoms as a causative factor (34). The data also support the conclusion of the Gluecks: "Mild neurotics, in whom the neurosis does not prevent the individual from efficient adaptation, also appear in lower proportion among the delinquents than among the nondelinquents (16.3% : 23.2%)" (26).

Perhaps unfortunately, the girls with 4 or 9 type profiles, who seem less likely to benefit from help, are frequently more interesting and likable as seen by the people who must choose who is to be offered help within our limited resources. Such girls seem at first to have many assets in contrast to the introverted, moody, neurotic-type girls who would be the better choice for intensive help according to these findings.

Three points should possibly be additionally emphasized. It is clear that the values of the MMPI for prediction cannot be derived from simple reading of individual scale elevations. Although several reliable differences between means could be established statistically among the individual scales in contrasting the poorer outcome cases with the good-outcome cases, the overlap was so great that it was not useful to look at one scale at a time. Instead, the profile analysis was arbitrarily dominated by the two scales showing the highest elevation in the profile. Thus it became at once clear, for example, that while scale 4 acting alone was an adverse scale, elevations of one or several other scales with favorable import along with the 4 tended to cancel out some of the adverse implication.

A second point that seemed apparent was that the mere elevation of the profile is not a completely dominant variable in the prediction. When, for example, scale 4 was elevated above other scales, but not so high as T score 70, it still constituted an indication that was almost as adverse as when the whole profile was higher and scale 4 went above 70.

The third point we should emphasize is that at least initial and final tests should be given during institutionalization. Attitudes and moods important to adjustment change often within a day, and certainly these change over a longer time. If this were not true, much of the purpose of the institutionalization system would be lost. It does not follow that we should expect the personality pattern observed at the time of release to be a more valid predictor. It might be too greatly a transient component of the institutional life. In a sense, if one had to choose, the admission personality could be argued to be the more real and lasting since the person is freshly from a real world. We believe that the best prediction might be attained from a test given after parole when the person is again in the real world. However, we have no data on this point.

The conclusions of this report are chiefly based upon treatment of the data emphasizing the profile pattern. This has been done in what we hope will soon be considered a primitive way. There are few statistical methods for profile treatment. It is not likely, for example, that all the available validity in an MMPI profile is packed into the two highest scale values. It is even possible that these carry a relatively small proportion of the validity. Yet this drastic simplification to combinations and permutations of one or two of the eight variables at a time left us still with 66 classes into which the observed profiles could have fallen and 43 different classes actually occurred among the 149 profiles analyzed.

CONCLUSIONS

1. Although a small number of delinquent girls obtained neurotic or psychotic types of MMPI profiles, none of these girls later showed severe enough behavior so that she became an institutional case for more than a brief period of time.

2. Two delinquent girls who later made tentative suicidal attempts both obtained mixed behavior and psychotic type MMPI profiles. Scales Pd and Sc were both prominent.

3. MMPI scales Hs, D, Hy, Pt, and even Pa and Sc, when dominant features in the profile configuration, occurred among relatively better

follow-up histories; but the best indication of good behavior was a profile with no codable high points.

4. MMPI scales Pd and Ma in combination and Pd alone as a dominant feature of a profile configuration were indicative of relatively bad follow-up histories.

5. Pooled prognostic judgments about the future social adjustment of the reform school girls as based upon the MMPI profiles appear significantly more correct than chance and are accurate enough to be useful. Such judgments must be made by experienced clinicians.

study 6

Personality Characteristics of Adolescents as Related to Their Later Careers . . .

PART I. INTRODUCTION AND GENERAL FINDINGS

BY STARKE R. HATHAWAY AND ELIO D. MONACHESI

THE general design of the studies introduced here was based upon large-scale objective personality testing of youngsters below the age where delinquency rates begin to climb rapidly, followed by repeated surveys to relate the earlier measures with later careers. We wished to do the initial survey in a manner that could be easily and cheaply reproduced if results should justify such testing of other populations.

Although we were well aware of possible shortcomings of the MMPI when applied to adolescents, we decided to adopt it as the survey instrument. This decision was based upon the fact that the MMPI possesses a fairly well established validity for adults; there are strong indications of its probable validity for juveniles; it contains 550 items suitable for item analysis; and new scales for it are continually being developed. Finally and most importantly, the MMPI is widely used and many professional people concerned with delinquency are familiar with it. These clinicians will be able to relate reports of findings to their own applications and connotations of the scales. This would seem to increase materially the value of the work as well as open the way to immediate practical or theoretical application.

The next problem involved the choice of a juvenile group for the initial survey. The advantages in favor of the selection of a single chronological age were outweighed by administrative difficulties. Instead, it was decided that all the children of a single school grade level should be chosen. The possible inappropriateness of some of the MMPI items for young children pointed to the desirability of selecting an upper grade. Yet the abrupt rise in the curve of incidence of juvenile delinquency, beginning at approximately age 14, restricted us to a grade composed of comparatively younger children. We decided on the ninth grade. The population of the study, then, was the public school ninth-grade children of Minneapolis, Minnesota.

Five high schools and eleven junior high schools in the Minneapolis public school system had ninth grades. The ninth grade of the University High School was also available for survey. The total enrollment of these schools in 1947–48 was 4572. Initial contacts with school administrative officers brought immediate cooperative interest in the proposed study.

In view of the possibility that there might be objections from parents or other sources to the content of a few of the MMPI items, one school was selected to serve as a trial run to determine what, if any, adverse reaction would develop. The school chosen for this purpose had a ninth-grade enrollment of 192 students. The principal, counselors, and teachers of this school became actively interested in the project and held meetings to aid in planning the testing program. The nature of the MMPI and the general purposes of the whole project were explained to the ninth-grade teachers, not only by the project personnel but also by the principal and school counselors, who were well informed.

Two class-hour periods were freed for the testing. It was decided to segregate boys and girls. A set of instructions was prepared which was to be read or clearly paraphrased to the pupils before the test. These instructions were as follows: "This is a test to study personality. The study is being made by the university and your records will be kept by them. No one will look at your answers to individual questions because the grades depend on counting up the marks only. The test has a great many statements about people, what they like, and what they think. It is used to aid in advising men and women about jobs and other problems. We want to see if it will be a help when taken by persons who are younger. So we are asking you to do it. You may find that some of the statements don't fit you at all, or they won't fit you until you are older. If you find any of these, answer them the best you can or leave them blank, but try to answer every statement. Work quickly but don't be careless. Some statements will be in the past tense, for example: 'My father was.' Answer as though in the present if your father is still living and you are with him."

After these instructions were read or given in an apparently extemporaneous way, the booklets and answer sheets were passed out. The answer sheet used for the test was the one printed for the "Engineers Northwest" (Hankes) scoring system. Directions are printed on the back of this answer sheet, and the boys and girls were told to read these and to feel free to ask for any other information they desired. Teachers and other supervisors were present in sufficient numbers to answer questions. The supervisors wandered about and unobtrusively watched for children who appeared to be in any way bewildered by the MMPI.

With this procedure it was found that the boys and girls in the trial school worked rapidly and surprisingly quietly after a few preliminary giggles and some attempts at intercommunication. Once really under way, very few pupils had any question about the MMPI items although it was common for one to inquire about the meaning of a word or whether or not he should answer in a particular way. To the latter type of questions, the examiners evaded a direct response.

The fastest pupils finished their papers in less than an hour. Nearly all were ready to leave in an hour and a half. The first ones to finish tended to speed up the slow ones by the act of leaving. A very few took as much time as was permitted and these were invited to come to the counselor's office to finish. (A shorter form of the MMPI may be used in the future for similar surveys. Most of the children would require only one class period to complete it.)

Upon completion of the testing program in the trial high school, all the papers were machine-scored; and a study was made to establish the percentage of invalid profiles and to discover any other irregularities in the answer sheets. While the F score was often rather high, nearly all the papers were answered with obvious validity.

The trial testing was completed about two weeks before the Christmas holidays began; and, during this two-week period, especially immediately following the administration of the test, teachers and counselors were on the alert to report any talk among the children or any other effects that might be related to the testing program. Four months were allowed to lapse before the testing phase of the study was conducted in other schools. Meanwhile, all concerned with the project in the trial school, as well as the project personnel, made every effort to discover any reactions of parents or others that would weigh against the use of the MMPI in the study of public school children. No disturbing events were reported. This was gratifying indeed, since the trial school drew its pupils from homes that differed more than is usual culturally, economically, and socially. This school, serving such a diversified community, had been selected in the first instance because it was believed that whatever adverse reaction the testing program would elicit from parents and other persons would be certain to materialize in this district.

Since everyone felt reassured by this initial testing, the broader survey was undertaken and all the remaining schools, with the exception of one where the principal and teachers objected to some of the items of the MMPI, were tested within two months, April and May of 1948. In most schools it proved impractical to separate boys and girls for the testing; it was quickly discovered, however, that this did not seem to affect the data adversely or raise other problems. Examiners universally reported that the children were less likely to show occasional facetious reactions or other evidences of concern to items we had feared might be embarrassing than to other items which no one had predicted would be attention-getting. On the whole, examiners, teachers, and counselors were more impressed by such examples of their inability to predict the children's reactions to the different items than by any adverse reaction relative to the content of the MMPI items.

Out of a total ninth-grade public school registration of 4572 pupils in Minneapolis, the testing program provided 4048 completed answer sheets. Two hundred and forty-one pupils were lost by the refusal of the one school to participate, and other pupils were absent from school on the day the tests were given or were prevented from taking the test by other incidental interferences. Many of these pupils were later tested, but some inevitably were not. The loss of two of these was especially dramatic. The two, while actually answering the test items, were summoned to the principal's office and thence to the city juvenile court for examination. They failed to complete the test. Needless to say, this loss of critical case material was keenly felt by the examiners who were in charge on that occasion!

The record blanks were machine-scored for all regular scales. These included ?, L, F, K, and the ten clinical scales. In addition to the regular scoring of the scales, the machine-scoring yielded sub-scores for obvious and subtle items as suggested by Wiener and Harmon (59). The profiles were drawn on the regular "Engineers Northwest" profile sheet. When this work was completed, the profiles were coded in accordance with the system developed by Hathaway (35). All clinical scales were numbered as usual with a zero representing the Si scale. The code was followed by a capital X when the L score was greater than 9 or when the F score was greater than 15. The X was used to indicate possible invalidity and should be interpreted as doing so within the meaning of the L and F scores. Unquestionably, many profiles with high L and F scores were really valid and some of them will be used for statistics in this study, but they will usually be specially treated. In all, only 266 codes (about 7 per cent) were marked X.

While the scoring and coding of the MMPI's were being completed, a microfilm apparatus was taken from school to school and the records kept by the school for each ninth-grader were microfilmed. These records included the cumulative record card and filed letters or other information pertaining to a given pupil. The cumulative record cards carried considerable information besides grades; in them were data about the family such as the occupation of the father and the number of brothers and sisters. The card also served as a health record and a dental hygiene record, and gave some facts regarding speech and reading disabilities. Scores for intelligence and educational tests were recorded. In addition, there were on the cards occasional notes by teachers regarding personality, special interests, or other characteristics of pupils, knowledge of which might prove useful to teachers in the school situation. Of course these records were frequently incomplete for students who had shifted from one school to another and some were inaccurate in detail. Intelligence test data often showed differences in accordance with the particular tests used and the different times the tests were administered.

Two file cards were next prepared for every pupil. One card carried the MMPI code and such identifying data as the school from which the pupil originated and the pupil's age. The other card carried the pupil's name and the MMPI code as a secondary entry. These cards were filed, the former in a code file numerically arranged so that profiles of any shape could immediately be found, and the latter alphabetically. Since many social data in agency records are filed according to the mother's or father's name rather than the pupil's name, it was also necessary to make complete lists from the photographic data of such identifying family information. This task was difficult because there were many inaccuracies in spelling and other errors. At the completion of this part of the project, most of the data collected were readily available.

RESULTS OF THE STUDY

In this study we are presenting only the general findings as a basis for a series of studies. We hope to obtain information about the early personality correlates of behavior problems and to estimate the predictive power of this objective personality test relative not alone to delinquency but also in later years to crime and mental disorders of a more severe nature. For follow-up data, it is planned that public records and other sources will be repeatedly surveyed to discover data on those ninth-graders who come into contact with therapeutic agencies or have personal difficulties of any type significant to this project. The results of the first follow-ups as they pertain to juvenile delinquency are given in Study 7 in this volume.

As indicated above, the whole ninth-grade population was 4572, of which 89 per cent were actually tested. We had for analysis 4048 records of which 1997 were male and 2051 female. Of these records, approximately 7 per cent were found to require special consideration because of deviant validity scale scores or because of incomplete records. Only 13 of these 266 cases were not usable because of too many "Cannot Say" responses, or because records were incomplete. Fifty boys and 42 girls, a total of about 2 per cent, answered ten or more of the L items in the direction indicating a tendency to put themselves in a satisfactory or socially desirable light. Approximately half of these answered ten and about one fifth answered eleven of the L items in the lie direction. There was a slight tendency for boys to obtain higher L scores.

Before the data were collected, we were uncertain how many of the children would understand the connotations of the words and phrases in the items so as to make their answers consistent with established scale validities. The degree to which our fears were apparently unfounded is partially indicated by the F scores. One hundred and three of the boys, representing about 5 per cent, obtained F scores that were in excess of a raw score of 15. Fifty-eight, or about 3 per cent, of the girls obtained similarly elevated F scores. Somewhat over 50 per cent of these elevated F scores for both the boys and girls were either 16, 17, or 18 raw score. These scores are not large enough to mean certain invalidity of the profile although, for some purposes, we shall eliminate records with such scores from statistical analysis.

In summary, high school children in the ninth grade, under the conditions that prevailed in this testing program, were found to be fairly cooperative and made reasonably consistent responses to the MMPI even though its original design was not influenced by the expectation that it would be administered to younger people.

Since adequate stability of certain statistics does not require numbers as large as those of our whole population, smaller samples of the boys and girls were selected to provide needed data. Two smaller samples, which will hereafter be referred to as the "correlation" samples, were made up of 200 boys and 200 girls. These two groups, although selected chiefly at random from among the whole populations, did fulfill two conditions which determined their inclusion in the correlation samples: (1) acceptable MMPI validity scores and (2) com-

plete cumulative school records. When any case, randomly chosen, did
not possess these characteristics, other cases were randomly selected
until the conditions for inclusion in the sample were met. Further, each
of the schools was represented in the correlation sample approximately
in proportion to the number of cases it had contributed to the entire
total of cases.

TABLE 1. AGE TO THE NEAREST WHOLE YEAR OF THE 200 BOYS
AND 200 GIRLS OF THE CORRELATION SAMPLE

Age	Percentage of Boys	Percentage of Girls
18	.0	.0
17	1.5	.0
16	24.5	9.5
15	58.0	65.5
14	15.5	25.0
13	.5	.0
12	.0	.0

Table 1 shows the age distribution for the correlation samples of
boys and girls and is representative of the age distribution of the
whole populations. The modal age is 15. The age range is slightly
greater for the boys than it is for the girls. (The individual ages were
rounded off to the nearest year.)

Table 2 gives the intercorrelation matrices for the correlation
samples. As has been indicated in previous papers, the correlation between scales 7 and 8 and that between scales 1 and 3 is high. A number
of other high correlations may be observed, most of which are consistent with routine interpretation of the variables correlated. As
would be expected, F and K are negatively correlated, as are scale 0
and K. Most of the correlations obtained between a given pair of
variables for boys were similar in size to corresponding pairs for girls.
Although some of the sex differences approach statistical significance,
we do not feel justified in attempting any interpretations.

After completion of profile coding for the whole population, median
T score profiles were obtained for the correlation groups and for each
of the schools. These median profiles were then coded and are presented in Table 3.

As will be noted, an additional group is introduced in Table 3. The
St. Cloud sample consists of the valid MMPI profiles of 101 boy and
81 girl ninth-graders of one high school in St. Cloud, Minnesota, tested
on November 15, 1948. This sample was added because of our desire

TABLE 2. INTERCORRELATION MATRICES OF THE VARIABLES AS OBTAINED ON THE
CORRELATION SAMPLES OF 200 FOR EACH SEX*

Scale	L	K	F	0 (Si)	1 (Hs) +.4K	2 (D)	3 (Hy)	4 (Pd) +.5K	5 (Mf)	6 (Pa)	7 (Pt) +1K	8 (Sc) +1K	9 (Ma) +.2K
L		.52	−.27	−.18	.09	.12	.10	−.12	.08	−.14	−.11	−.12	−.25
K	.44		−.44	−.52	.22	.07	.32	.11	.03	−.08	−.01	−.07	−.25
F	−.19	−.42		.28	.22	.16	.06	.36	−.12	.30	.41	.57	.44
0 (Si)	.07	−.27	.23		.09	.43	−.01	.05	.07	.13	.37	.24	−.19
1 (Hs) +.4K	.26	.45	.06	.04		.41	.69	.38	.03	.29	.43	.50	.08
2 (D)	.22	.08	.16	.35	.42		.44	.41	.24	.27	.40	.36	−.12
3 (Hy)	.28	.45	.03	−.10	.73	.43		.39	.15	.31	.32	.38	−.04
4 (Pd) +.5K	.01	.27	.29	−.03	.38	.24	.40		−.09	.42	.46	.54	.33
5 (Mf)	−.08	−.05	.04	.10	.22	.31	.33	.15		.05	.09	−.06	−.23
6 (Pa)	−.16	−.14	.39	.11	.19	.23	.22	.26	.33		.42	.53	.18
7 (Pt) +1K	−.07	.11	.29	.32	.46	.50	.42	.44	.25	.42		.75	.35
8 (Sc) +1K	−.10	.08	.40	.19	.43	.29	.38	.44	.30	.49	.68		.50
9 (Ma) +.2K	−.35	−.23	.30	−.09	−.11	−.19	−.06	.27	.08	.26	.09	.31	

*The italic correlation coefficients are for boys, the roman for girls.

TABLE 3. CODES OF THE MEDIAN PROFILES OF THE VARIOUS SAMPLES

(The numbers in parentheses are the T values of the highest and
lowest points on the given profile.)

Samples	Boys	Girls
St. Cloud	'489 27– (62;49)	'458 70– (57;50)
Correlation group	'9487– (58;49)	'45789– (60;47)
School A	'8497– (61;51)	'58 49– (57;46)
School B	'498– (60;48)	'9458– (60;46)
School C	'49 87– (60;48)	'5489– (57;46)
School D	'48359– (57;50)	'4–1 (57;44)
School E	'498– (62;49)	'49857– (60;49)
School F	'4987– (62;49)	'9845– (63;47)
School G	'489 73– (60;50)	'4859– (60;46)
School H	'8947– (57;49)	'45–12 (55;45)
School I	'489– (62;49)	'45– (55;46)
School J	'498– (60;47)	'048759– (58;46)
School K	'498– (60;49)	'4589– (55;46)
School L	'9487– (58;50)	'48– (57;46)
School M	'4987– (60;49)	'48 579– (57;46)
School N	'48973– (60;51)	'48– (57;47)
School O	'489– (60;50)	'9485– (58;46)
School P	'9487– (63;48)	'8479– (57;46)

to obtain MMPI data on some rural ninth-grade school children. At
least one third of the pupils in this sample were from rural homes and
the remainder were from a much smaller urban center than those of
the larger sample.

An examination of Table 3 will indicate that, although there is some
variation in order, all the median profiles for the boys show variables
4, 8, and 9 as the three highest points. These scales are respectively Pd,
Sc, and Ma. Scale 7 is the next most frequent elevation and 5 and 3
occasionally occur. The highest T score value observed on any of
these median profiles is 63. No profile point occurs as a T score median
below 47 on any of the male groups. Among the codes for the girls, 4 is
the most frequent high point as was true for the boys. There is, however, somewhat greater variability and a tendency for the profiles to
be slightly less elevated. Also, in two of the profiles, scale 1 is as low
as a T of 45 or below; in one of these two profiles, scale 2 is also at that
value. One would seem justified in saying that, within this population
and the test validity, the girls obtain scores indicating better adjustment as interpreted through the adult norms that determined the T
values. As will be more clearly brought out by later data, variable 5 is
a frequent high point among the female groups, indicating a masculine
pattern of interests. Although some of the differences in profiles from

one school to another approached or actually reached statistical reliability, the absolute values of the differences are so small that for the present at least it is inadvisable to attempt any interpretations.

When we turn to the whole array of median profiles, certain patterns stand out. If responses to items of scale 4 may be interpreted as manifestations of a tendency toward rebellion and if those of scale 9 may be considered to indicate enthusiasm and varying directions of activity, then these profiles would seem to support common ideas about the psychology of the high school pupil. Certainly there does not seem to be much depression; the only profile with scale 2 as a coded high point is that of the St. Cloud boys. The tendency for scale 8 also to be elevated is temptingly reminiscent of the fact that the first episode in schizophrenic case histories so often occurs during youth. This score may gain in significance as our cases are followed into adult life. It is interesting that in both boys and girls the neurotic elements indicated by the neurotic triad (scales 1, 2, and 3) are not conspicuous. The neurotic scale 7 is, however, more often elevated. If we may make the point without undue emphasis, it would seem that these median profiles tend in the direction of behavior disorders or of psychotic trends rather than toward neurotic patterns. Also, the more characteristic neurotic elements of youth tend to be in the direction of obsessive compulsive phobic states as seen in psychasthenia.

Another way in which the characteristic high school pupils' MMPI profiles may be presented is shown in Tables 4 and 5. In these tables will be found the percentage frequency of occurrence of high and low points as observed among the total number of boys and girls obtaining apparently valid profiles. An illustration of how to read these tables may be drawn from Table 4. If we begin in the upper left corner of the table, we see that .05 per cent of the profiles were found to be without any codable high or low point. That would mean that in these profiles no one of the ten scales exceeded a T score of 54 or fell below a T score of 46. Of all observed profiles, .82 per cent had variable 0, which is Si, occurring above all other points and at a T value greater than 54 but no point below a T of 46. Similarly, the remaining values given across the top line show the frequency of occurrence of each of the scales as a highest point on the profiles where no scale was coded as a low point. The next line shows the frequency of occurrence of each high scale in profiles where variable 0 was coded as a low point. And so on.

In Table 4 we can also see that the most characteristic combination of coded high and low points for boys was 9–2, with 6.80 per cent of all

TABLE 4. RELATIVE FREQUENCIES OF VARIOUS COMBINATIONS OF INITIAL SCALES IN THE HIGH-POINT CODES OF THE NINTH-GRADE BOYS WITH THE INITIAL SCALES OF THE LOW-POINT CODES

(Figures are in percentages of the 1836 codes.)

Low Scale	High Scale											
	–	0	1	2	3	4	5	6	7	8	9	Total
–	.05	.82	1.43	1.26	.99	6.36	.93	1.26	2.80	5.37	2.96	24.23
0	.00		.44	.16	.71	2.74	.66	.16	.16	.99	2.19	8.22
1	.11	.88		.33	.00	1.26	.82	.55	.49	1.37	2.96	8.77
2	.99	.38	.22		.44	3.02	1.48	.44	.33	1.86	6.80	15.95
3	.11	.82	.00	.27		1.04	.27	.16	.66	1.32	2.91	7.57
4	.05	.49	.05	.33	.00		.27	.11	.16	.44	.33	2.25
5	.22	.49	.49	.82	.27	4.17		.44	1.04	2.03	3.13	13.10
6	.33	.77	.33	.55	.22	2.63	.55		.44	1.26	1.59	8.66
7	.27	.11	.11	.22	.05	.49	.22	.11		.16	.99	2.74
8	.22	.22	.00	.16	.00	.11	.16	.00	.05		.11	1.04
9	.16	.82	.60	1.21	.60	1.75	1.04	.33	.44	.49		7.46
Total	2.51	5.81	3.67	5.32	3.29	23.57	6.41	3.56	6.58	15.30	23.96	100.00

TABLE 5. RELATIVE FREQUENCIES OF VARIOUS COMBINATIONS OF INITIAL SCALES IN THE HIGH-POINT CODES OF THE NINTH-GRADE GIRLS WITH THE INITIAL SCALES OF THE LOW-POINT CODES

(Figures are in percentages of the 1946 codes.)

Low Scale	High Scale											
	–	0	1	2	3	4	5	6	7	8	9	Total
–		.88	.21	.10	.67	5.31	1.19	1.24	1.19	2.42	1.86	15.05
0	.15		.00	.00	.52	1.70	.62	.41	.26	.26	1.08	5.00
1	.46	3.09		.10	.21	3.20	2.73	1.24	1.03	1.44	4.23	17.73
2	.26	.82	.05		1.08	3.97	5.15	1.80	.62	1.50	5.67	20.93
3	.21	2.06	.00	.05		1.08	2.22	.52	.21	1.19	1.86	9.38
4	.21	.57	.05	.00	.00		.77	.31	.10	.05	.05	2.11
5	.15	.77	.05	.21	.52	2.58		1.03	.67	.93	1.29	8.20
6	.26	1.44	.10	.21	.21	1.44	2.27		.26	.52	1.29	7.99
7	.15	.05	.05	.05	.05	.67	.72	.15		.00	.21	2.11
8	.00	.15	.00	.05	.00	.05	.05	.05	.00		.00	.36
9	.36	2.78	.21	.36	.67	2.01	3.09	.72	.62	.31		11.13
Total	2.21	12.63	.72	1.13	3.92	22.01	18.81	7.47	4.95	8.61	17.53	100.00

male profiles having Ma as the highest coded point and D as the lowest coded point. Next in frequency was the pattern 4– which made up 6.36 per cent of all valid profiles. These 4– profiles had Pd as the highest coded point and no T score low enough to be coded. Another frequent combination was 8–, which occurred with a frequency of 5.37. In these profiles, Sc was highest and no point was low enough to be coded. Several of the possible combinations were not observed at all and others were very infrequent. For example, Hy as a high point and

Sc as a low point (the combination 3–8) did not occur among the 1836 cases. This is more surprising in view of the fact that in Table 2 these variables show a correlation of only .38 and this low correlation should certainly permit enough independent variability for us to observe one quite high when the other is low. We cannot yet tell if the tendency for these boys to get higher scores on Sc is validly related to the clinical syndrome of schizophrenia. The median profiles showed the same trend.

Table 5 gives similar frequency values for the girls. Although many of the frequencies are similar to those observed among the boys, there are marked differences. As with the boys, a common combination was 9–2, but the relative frequency of the combination 5–2 was markedly higher than among the boys. This tendency, for Mf to be elevated among the girls, might be the result of T table distortion, or it might indicate a masculine protest. The data do not provide a way to discriminate among these and other possibilities. We can only say that it would be consistent with the findings of many who have studied the adolescent girl if it were established psychometrically that she shows a more masculine pattern than a comparable group of older women.

Figures 1 and 2 show the relative frequency of occurrence of the various pairs of high points among the codes. The N used to calculate the percentage values was the number of codes that were not X codes. The codes with underlined scales in the first two places (12...–) are evenly distributed in the two permutations (12...– and 21...–). Codes with the second and third scales underlined (123...–) are divided between the two combinations (12 and 13). Codes with the second and two or more following scales underlined are classified without regard to the underlining (1234...– would be called a 12). Codes having the first three or more scales underlined are listed as indeterminate (?). Codes with no high point are indicated by a dash (–).

For both boys and girls the high frequency of combinations with 9, particularly 94 and 98, is at once apparent. Other similarly common high-point combinations are 48 and 49. It would seem reasonable enough that the high school child should be characteristically hypomanic in contrast to adult behavior. Certainly, projected against such adult behavior, the high school child is interested in many things, and many of his active interests are transient though marked with enthusiasm. In these characteristics he is similar to the clinical case who becomes hypomanic. Variable 4, representing similarity to the older psychopathic deviate person, is probably here an expression of the widespread revolt that is frequently said to be characteristic of the transition from childhood into adulthood. Insofar as the items in the

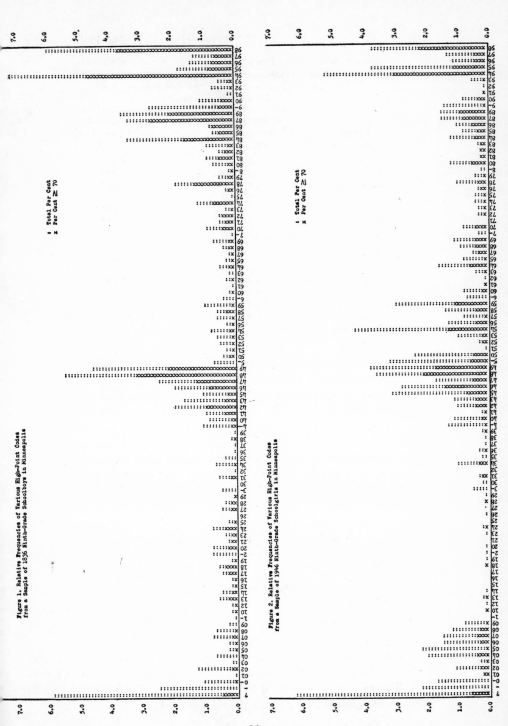

Figure 1. Relative Frequencies of Various High-Point Codes
from a Sample of 1836 Ninth-Grade Schoolboys in Minneapolis

Figure 2. Relative Frequencies of Various High-Point Codes
from a Sample of 1946 Ninth-Grade Schoolgirls in Minneapolis

: Total Per Cent
x Per Cent ≥ 70

TABLE 6. SOME OF THE PERCENTAGES SHOWING SIGNIFICANT DIFFER-
ENCES BETWEEN SEXES ON THE FREQUENCY OF OCCURRENCE OF
THE VARIOUS SCALES IN THE FIRST POSITION OF THE
HIGH-POINT CODES

Coded High Points	Percentage of Ninth-Grade Boys, N = 1836	Percentage of Ninth-Grade Girls, N = 1946
0	5.9	12.6**
04	.7	2.0**
04 and 40	1.6	3.1**
05	.3	2.2**
05 and 50	.7	4.6**
06 and 60	.5	2.3**
1	3.2**	.6
2	4.3**	.8
24 and 42	2.8**	1.2
42	2.0**	1.0
45	1.1	3.1**
45 and 54	1.9	7.4**
46 and 64	2.5	4.4**
47 and 74	3.8**	2.1
48	5.5**	3.6
48 and 84	8.9**	4.8
49 and 94	11.8**	9.0
5	5.6	17.6**
5−	.7	3.2**
50	.4	2.4**
54	.8	4.3**
56 and 65	.6	2.1**
59	1.0	3.0**
59 and 95	2.8	6.7**
6	3.2	7.0**
78 and 87	5.3**	2.5
8	15.2**	8.1
84	3.4**	1.2
87	3.4**	1.5
89	3.6**	1.5
89 and 98	9.6**	5.2
9	22.9**	18.0
9−	2.7**	1.4
95	1.8	3.7**
98	6.0**	3.7

**Signifies the larger percentage of a difference reliable above
the 1 per cent level of confidence.

Pd scale would reflect conflict with family or society, we might expect
that the adolescent would score high on the Pd scale.

Table 6 shows the percentages yielding some of the larger differences
between the sexes in the frequency of the highest points of the profiles. The examples chosen for the table all showed a difference significant with a probability greater than 1 per cent.

Scales 0, 5, and 6 were more frequent high points among the girls and 1, 2, 8, and 9 among the boys. Insofar as they are valid, these findings indicate that girls encounter greater difficulty in making social adjustments, reacting with masculine protest and paranoid sensitivity.

In Table 7 some of the percentages yielding large and reliable dif-

TABLE 7. THE MORE IMPORTANT PERCENTAGES YIELDING DIFFERENCES IN FREQUENCY OF THE TOP CODE POINTS FOR NINTH-GRADERS COMPARED TO COLLEGE LIBERAL ARTS FRESHMEN

Coded High Points	Percentage of Ninth-Grade Boys, N = 1836	Percentage of College Boys,[a] N = 607	Percentage of Ninth-Grade Girls, N = 1946	Percentage of College Girls,[a] N = 517
2	4.3	5.6	.8	3.3 **
3	2.7	7.3 **	2.9	12.0 **
34	.6	2.1 **	1.0	2.7
4	22.4 **	14.2	19.6 **	11.6
45	1.1	2.1	3.1 **	.2
48	5.5 **	1.3	3.6 **	.8
5	5.6	24.8 **	17.6 **	7.9
50	.4	2.1 **	2.4	.8
52	.5	2.0 **	.3	.2
53	.6	2.8 **	1.0	.8
54	.8	3.0 **	4.3 **	.8
56	.3	2.0 **	1.3	.2
57	.6	2.8 **	.8	.2
58	.6	2.8 **	1.4	1.0
59	1.0	4.3 **	3.0	1.4
6	3.2	2.6	7.0	12.4 **
8	15.2 **	7.4	8.1	6.8
84	3.4 **	1.0	1.2	1.2
87	3.4 **	1.3	1.5	1.9
9-	2.7	3.0	1.4	3.7 **
93	.5	1.0	.5	3.5 **
95	1.8	5.8 **	3.7	2.1
98	6.0 **	3.3	3.7	2.7

** Signifies the larger of the two percentages yielding a difference reliable above the 1 per cent level of confidence.

[a] The data on the college students are from the Counseling Bureau, University of Minnesota, by courtesy of Charles W. Goulding.

ferences between ninth-graders and college freshmen are presented. The college students were tested at about the time of college entrance when they were registering for a liberal arts curriculum. The college boys show a markedly greater tendency to have 5 as the highest profile point. Possibly this femininity of interests is related to a selective action of the liberal arts curriculum and would not hold for engineering registrants, for example. But we suspect the more masculine boys are less likely to go to college. Although the trend was not nearly so clear, the college girls also tended to be more feminine. They showed lesser frequency of a high 5. We have already pointed out, however, that the ninth-grade girls were relatively deviant on Mf so this present datum indicates a moderate change toward the adult average. When all profiles with a high 6 scale are counted (6...), the college girls show a greater frequency of such profiles. At these moderate levels of elevation the score probably indicates greater social sensitivity. Both sexes of the college samples show some tendency toward larger scores on scale 3, which could mean a greater average tendency toward naiveté and other psychological characteristics similar to the hysterias. Finally, the ninth-grade boys obtain a significantly greater frequency of high 8 profiles. If this latter relates to a greater susceptibility for schizoid symptoms, it would appear that the boys who drop out of school must be those with this tendency at its strongest.

Table 8 shows the code frequencies of the ninth-graders as contrasted to our samples of adult normal married persons. Tables 9 and 10 show the means and standard deviations for the correlation groups

TABLE 8. THE MORE IMPORTANT PERCENTAGES YIELDING DIFFERENCES IN FREQUENCY OF THE TOP CODE POINTS FOR NINTH-GRADERS COMPARED TO ADULT MARRIED NORMALS

Coded High Points	Percentage of Ninth-Grade Boys, N = 1836	Percentage of Male Adults, N = 258	Percentage of Ninth-Grade Girls, N = 1946	Percentage of Female Adults, N = 360
–	4.6	23.6**	9.6	25.8**
1	3.6	10.6**	.8	8.7**
13	.7	3.5**	.3	3.9**
2	6.0	6.7	2.5	12.5**
21	.6	.8	.0	2.5**
27	1.0	.8	.3	3.3**
3	3.6	7.1	3.8	7.7**
31	.7	1.6	.4	3.1**
4	24.1**	11.6	26.0**	8.4
46	2.3**	.0	3.9**	1.1
47	2.8**	.4	3.1**	.6
48	6.1**	1.9	5.2**	.3
49	5.3**	1.9	5.7**	1.1
8	16.7**	5.2	11.3**	6.2
87	4.5**	.4	2.8	1.1
89	4.2**	.4	2.4	1.1
9	24.7**	17.6	22.7**	13.1
9–	4.0	9.3**	5.3	7.5
94	8.3**	4.3	7.2**	2.2
98	6.9**	.8	5.9**	.8

**Signifies the larger of the two percentages yielding a difference reliable above the 1 per cent level of confidence.

TABLE 9. MEANS AND STANDARD DEVIATIONS OF THE NINTH-GRADE BOYS CONTRASTED TO MMPI STANDARDIZATION GROUPS

Scale	Ninth-Grade Boys				MMPI Standardization Males[a]				
	N	Mean T	Mean Raw	SD Raw	N	Mean T	Mean Raw	SD Raw	D
L	200	48.0	3.6	2.06	294	50.0	4.1	2.89	-2.0*
F	200	57.0	5.8	3.66	111	50.0	3.9	4.24	7.0**
K	200	54.0	14.2	4.78	274	52.6	13.5	5.66	1.4
0 (Si)	200	51.4	26.2	7.62	193	50.0	25.0	9.58	1.4
1 (Hs)	200	50.4	11.5	3.32	274	50.0	11.3	3.90	0.4
2 (D)	200	52.0	17.5	4.13	294	50.0	16.6	4.18	2.0*
3 (Hy)	200	51.7	17.4	4.14	342	50.0	16.5	5.51	1.7*
4 (Pd)	200	59.5	22.9	4.42	274	51.0	19.3	4.11	8.5**
5 (Mf)	200	52.3	21.6	4.50	117	50.0	20.4	5.13	2.3*
6 (Pa)	200	52.9	9.0	3.22	293	50.1	8.1	3.56	2.8**
7 (Pt)	200	56.2	26.0	4.80	274	50.0	22.9	4.88	6.2**
8 (Sc)	200	59.1	27.0	5.21	274	50.0	22.3	5.21	9.1**
9 (Ma)	200	59.5	20.6	4.11	274	50.0	17.0	3.87	9.5**

* Signifies a difference reliable above the 5 per cent level of confidence.
** Signifies a difference reliable above the 1 per cent level of confidence.
[a] The standardization groups consisted of general population adults except for Si. Si data were taken from the sample used by Drake (13).

TABLE 10. MEANS AND STANDARD DEVIATIONS OF THE NINTH-GRADE GIRLS CONTRASTED TO MMPI STANDARDIZATION GROUPS

Scale	Ninth-Grade Girls				MMPI Standardization Females[a]				D
	N	Mean T	Mean Raw	SD Raw	N	Mean T	Mean Raw	SD Raw	
L	200	49.0	3.8	2.09	397	50.0	4.3	2.63	−1.0*
F	200	55.0	5.1	3.39	118	50.0	3.5	3.13	5.0**
K	200	54.0	14.2	2.92	373	50.0	12.1	5.07	4.0**
0 (Si)	200	53.0	27.8	7.44	350	50.0	25.0	9.58	3.0**
1 (Hs)	200	48.0	12.3	3.68	373	50.0	13.1	4.88	−2.0*
2 (D)	200	48.0	18.3	4.00	396	50.0	19.3	5.18	−2.0**
3 (Hy)	200	51.0	19.3	4.53	475	50.0	18.8	5.66	1.0
4 (Pd)	200	60.0	23.0	4.33	373	49.0	18.4	4.40	11.0**
5 (Mf)	200	56.0	33.8	4.39	108	50.0	36.5	4.83	6.0**
6 (Pa)	200	50.0	8.0	3.28	397	50.0	8.0	3.92	0.0
7 (Pt)	200	54.0	27.9	4.80	373	50.0	25.2	6.06	4.0**
8 (Sc)	200	57.0	27.2	5.74	373	50.0	22.7	6.50	7.0**
9 (Ma)	200	56.0	19.3	4.32	373	48.0	16.1	4.11	8.0**

* Signifies a difference reliable above the 5 per cent level of confidence.
** Signifies a difference reliable above the 1 per cent level of confidence.
[a] The standardization groups consisted of general population adults except for Si. Si data were taken from the sample used by Drake (13).

as compared to the original MMPI standard statistics. The adults came from the original cross-section population of Minnesota. Unfortunately, Si and Mf could not be scored for the adults so all codes had to be written and redistributed without scales 0 and 5 to obtain data for Table 8. If low T scores on the eight scales mean better adjustment, the adults are, in several ways, a little better adjusted. They obtain many more profiles with no T score above 54 (profiles having no high points coded and signified by –), and the mean scores on 4, 7, 8, and 9 are definitely lower. Adults, however, do show a greater tendency to obtain high neurotic scores (1..., 2..., and 3..., codes having Hy, D, or Hs as the highest coded point). With the exception of 9– (codes with Ma as the only score above T of 54) the ninth-graders show higher percentages for all the other significant differences. Of especial note is the marked frequency of 4... (all profiles having Pd as the highest coded point). As stated above, this perhaps reflects conflict with the family. Also characteristic of the ninth-graders are higher scores on variables 8 and 9. Ma is to be expected, as noted in Figures 1 and 2, but the higher value of Sc characteristic of the boys, not as clear in the figures, is more obvious here. The data on the college samples likewise showed 8 lower than among ninth-graders, so the schizoid trends seem to be restricted to the adolescents.

Among the data recorded for each child was the rent level of the city block in which his home was located. These rent levels were determined as of 1940, and four rent ranges of about equal frequency were used as a four-category variable. A comparison of the MMPI profiles of children living in the highest and the lowest of these four rent-level groups was made. Table 11 shows the relative frequencies of the various highest points on the profiles for the combinations where one

TABLE 11. THE LARGER CONTRASTING FREQUENCIES OF HIGHEST CODED POINTS ON MMPI PROFILES OF CHILDREN FROM HIGH-RENT BLOCKS AND CHILDREN FROM LOW-RENT BLOCKS

Coded High Points	High Rent		Low Rent	
	Boys, N = 197	Girls, N = 228	Boys, N = 340	Girls, N = 353
46 and 64	1.0	1.3	1.5	4.8*
48	1.5	3.5	4.7*	3.7
4	13.7	18.1	24.4*	20.0
59 and 95	6.6*	6.1	1.5	7.3
8	15.7	5.7	17.4	11.3*

*Signifies the larger of the two differences showing a difference between the rent levels reliable above the 5 per cent level of confidence.

of the observed frequency differences was at the 5 per cent or better probability level.

Differences shown in Table 11 are not very impressive but could be deeply significant of trends. In part the differences are attenuated by the crudity of estimated rent levels of blocks in measuring the socio-economic placement of individual families. In any case, rent level as here observed is not an important factor in determining code frequencies. There tends to be more 2 and 4 dominance among low-rent children and more 3, 5, and 9 among high-rent children.

TABLE 12. CORRELATIONS (SYMMETRICAL SURFACE) BETWEEN VARIA-
BLES OBTAINED FOR TWENTY-SIX PAIRS OF TWINS AND THIRTY
PAIRS OF UNLIKE AGE SIBLINGS AND, FOR COMPARISON, TEST-
RETEST CORRELATIONS FROM THE CAPWELL STUDY

Scale	Twins, N = 26	Brothers and Sisters, N = 30	Public School Girls Test-Retest, N = 55
L	.46**	−.17	.48**
K	.63**	−.08	.66**
F	.59**	.36*	.51**
0 (Si)	.46**	.11	
1 (Hs)	.00	.31	.59**
2 (D)	.23	.18	.51**
3 (Hy)	.12	.16	.52**
4 (Pd)	.43**	.01	.46**
5 (Mf)	.32	.15	
6 (Pa)	.25	.15	.50**
7 (Pt)	.15	.09	.48**
8 (Sc)	.17	.24	.60**
9 (Ma)	.31	−.07	.55**

*Signifies a correlation reliable above the 5 per cent level of confidence.
**Signifies a correlation reliable above the 1 per cent level of confidence.

Table 12 gives data on an incidental line of investigation made possible by the large sample tested. Twenty-six pairs of children were found to have identical last names and birthdays. It was assumed that these were twins, but we did not attempt to determine how many of them were identical twins. There were four male pairs, thirteen female pairs, and nine mixed pairs. The data for these twenty-six pairs were treated with a formula for symmetrical surface correlation and the highest correlation was observed for K; F was almost as high; and L, 0, and 4 were significantly correlated.

In order to obtain comparative data, thirty pairs of children with identical last names and residences were chosen on the assumption that they were siblings. Five of these pairs were boys, ten were girls, and fifteen were mixed. For these, similar correlations showed a tendency toward positive correlation; but none of the correlations was large. As a final comparison, fifty-five public high school girls from the study by Capwell were assumed to provide somewhat comparable test-retest correlations on most of the variables, although Capwell's second tests were given after an interval of approximately nine months.

The K variable is often thought to reflect socio-economic status and other cultural backgrounds. Common cultural influences could have, in whole or part, determined these data; but there is not sufficient proof yet to justify selection of either culture or heredity as the prime factor. The data of Table 12 are by no means stable enough to permit definitive conclusions, but they offer provocative implications; and we feel that these twin and sibling groups may afford some of the most interesting data in later follow-up studies. The fact that there are larger correlations between some MMPI variables as the degree of familial relationship increases is in support of the findings of Gjerdi (22).

SUMMARY

The city-wide testing of ninth-grade public school children in sixteen schools in a large city and one school in a smaller city has demonstrated that it is practical to administer the MMPI to children of this age level. Little difficulty was encountered when the testing was conducted in a professional and objective manner.

The majority of the profiles supplied by the project appeared to be rational and although the MMPI was initially expected to be poorly adapted to the age level of the children, they, in fact, experienced no great difficulty in handling the items. What actually occurred during the testing indicated that we were unable to predict accurately which items would be misunderstood or might create anxiety in the children. It was believed that some of the sex items might be embarrassing and troublesome; such, however, did not prove to be the case, perhaps because of the fact that the sex items were few in number and scattered among other items.

Findings of more significance will not be available until the subsequent histories are traced. Interpretations made of the descriptive data presented must, at this point, depend chiefly upon the assumption that the validity of the various scales of the MMPI based upon adult clinical cases carries over to the present subjects. Some published data, as well as our clinical experience, tend to support this assumption; nevertheless, its complete reliability must await follow-up data.

If, for the moment, we may assume that such validity exists, several group trends appear in the scores. Boys and girls differed significantly on certain scales. The boys were more schizoid (scale 8) and had a greater tendency to be overactive (scale 9) and rebellious (scale 4). The girls were much more socially introverted (scale 0) and sensitive (scale 6). There was a definite relative masculinity of interest among the girls (scale 5).

In contrast to ninth-graders, college boys were more feminine (scale 5) and less schizoid (scale 8). College girls showed still greater tendency toward social sensitivity (scale 6) and a little more neuroticism (scales 2 and 3) than did the ninth-graders.

When contrasted with general population adults, several large average differences appeared. The ninth-graders were more like obsessive-compulsive (scale 7), schizophrenic (scale 8), and hypomanic (scale 9) patients than were the adults. In profile patterns these trends were supplemented by a tendency for the aggressive or rebellious pattern to dominate the profiles of the ninth-graders (scales 4 and 9). This comparison also indicated that the neurotic scales (scales 1, 2, and 3) assumed more prominence in the profiles of adults. There were a significantly smaller number of moderately elevated profiles (no high point coded) among adults, suggesting an over-all better adjustment.

When children from high-rent areas were compared to those from low-rent areas, the high-rent boys were somewhat more manic and feminine (scales 9 and 5), the low-rent boys more aggressive and schizoid (scales 4 and 8). The low-rent girls were more aggressive and socially sensitive (scales 4 and 6) and also more schizoid (scale 8).

Finally, twenty-six pairs of twins showed that there was a fairly strong tendency toward positive correlations between the scores of the pairs on various scales. Scores for scales L, K, F, 4, and 0 yielded significant correlations; the largest of these had a value of .63 and was obtained from the K scores. Correlations for thirty pairs of non-twin siblings were smaller, but showed similar trends. For several variables, correlations between twins approached test-retest correlation in size. Although these data do not prove the existence of a causal relation between these personality scores and degree of similarity of heredity or environment, they are at least consistent with and suggestive of such relationship.

study 7

Personality Characteristics of Adolescents as Related to Their Later Careers . . .

PART II. TWO-YEAR FOLLOW-UP ON DELINQUENCY

BY STARKE R. HATHAWAY AND ELIO D. MONACHESI

I<small>N JANUARY</small> 1950, two years after the time of testing the ninth-graders, a check of the records of the Hennepin County Probation Office and the Juvenile Division of the Minneapolis Police Department was begun. The median age of these youngsters was now 17. The purpose of this investigation was to determine who of the children had appeared on the official records within or before the two-year interval. The search revealed that 591 of those with completed profiles had appeared before the court, the police, or both; 22 per cent of all the boys and 8 per cent of all the girls were among these.

Three arbitrary levels of antisocial difficulty were set up, and as each name was discovered in the records during this limited follow-up, a rating was made according to the level at which the youngster seemed to have been involved. Since we felt that it was impossible to set up a rigorous definition of these levels and that it was more important to achieve consistency than to attempt elaborate classification by setting values on each of the numerous types of offense, these ratings were made by the junior scientist who studied the record, on the basis of her assessment of the case as she read the available material. The following descriptions of behavior characteristics of each of the three levels are therefore generalized and are given to illustrate broadly the level represented by each class. The first level represents persons who are unquestionably referable as delinquents; the third is so mild as to

EDITORS' NOTE. The discrepancies to be noted between previously published results pertaining to the topics discussed in this paper and the results contained herein are due to the acquisition of additional data since the initial follow-up (January 1950 to July 1950) was completed. Such data necessitated corrections in classification of some cases, thus changing several published findings. In general, however, the results presented do not differ from published results in any significant fashion.

include few persons who could legitimately be called delinquent, at least on the basis of the available information.

I. This level of misconduct is used to denote those who committed repeated offenses such as auto theft, burglary, grand larceny, holdup with a gun, and gross immoral conduct (girls), accompanied by less serious offenses. In this category were placed all youngsters who were considered to have demonstrated a well-established delinquent pattern.

II. This classification involves the commission of only one serious offense such as auto theft, grand larceny, or gross immorality, or more than one less serious offense such as petty larceny, immoral conduct, assault, disorderly conduct, malicious destruction of property, shoplifting, flagrant curfew violations, truancy, and incorrigibility. The youngsters placed in this class were therefore not clearly established as delinquent, but nevertheless they were showing behavior that needed more than casual explanation.

III. The youngsters placed in this class had committed minor offenses such as destruction of property (especially when this was connected with play activities), drinking, one or more traffic offenses (escapades involving speeding, driving without a license, and/or going at high speed through a stop light or sign), curfew violation, and immoral conduct. The misbehavior was relatively nondelinquent in comparison to that of the other two categories. Nevertheless, these children as a group were considered to have demonstrated disquieting evidence of undesirable conduct.

The reader should keep in mind that although the offenses leading to the registration of a name are, in many cases, minor ones, it is an unwritten policy of the police to overlook a given offense if the child shows immediate evidences of contrition and the whole affair appears within reasonable limits. In general, a juvenile does not readily get his name on the police record even for breaking windows unless, when the authorities come to know of the affair, there is evidence that indicates a degree of maliciousness or unrepentant rebellion.

In the discussions and data that follow, the youngsters classified in any one of these three categories will be referred to as delinquents. The reader should modify this use of the word as he sees fit. It is not intended to brand the class III youngsters as definitely delinquent; but some word is needed to refer generally to those who get their names into the police records, and we feel that this word will serve the purpose although it is used loosely. We are certain that many of the youngsters of levels II and III will not again have contact with the authorities; we are equally confident, however, that further follow-up will show that some class III youths have gone on to more severe misbehavior.

In addition to classifying the cases discovered in this follow-up according to the severity of their behavior, the same cases, where possible, were also classified according to whether the first definite offenses occurred before the time of testing in the ninth grade, after the time of testing, or both before and after. These three groups were called respectively A, the after-testing group, B, the before-testing group, and C, the continuous delinquency group where the record included misbehavior both before and after the time of testing. If we are most properly to speak of prediction of delinquency, the A group, whose offenses occurred after testing, presents the best available data. In the evidence they yield, the B and C groups are somewhat more similar to groups used in other studies where testing has occurred after the delinquency has begun. But in the present studies the testing was done in a completely separate setting during the routine school year. For this reason even the cases classed as B or C are of more theoretical interest than if they had been tested in an institution or in a parole or probationary situation.

As stated above, the follow-up revealed that 22 per cent of the boys from whom an MMPI record was obtained at the time of the general testing of ninth-graders had their names registered in the juvenile probation office or the police department files. The codes of a substantial number of these boys showed high L or F scores. When these invalid records were removed from the sample, the delinquents among the remainder constituted 20 per cent of all the sample.

It is quite significant that of the total 161 invalid records obtained from the whole sample of 1997 boys, 37 per cent became delinquent in the present sense. Contrasting this to the 20 per cent rate for valid records, a priori it would seem that one of the more important factors making for MMPI invalidity among the records from boys is also related to the commission of delinquent acts; the delinquency rate among boys who invalidated their MMPI records was about 85 per cent greater than the rate among boys who obtained acceptable validity scores in the testing. This trend was also present among the girls although the numbers are too small to make the findings reliable. Only 7 per cent of the girls with clearly valid records were registered by the authorities, but of the 105 girls with invalid profiles from the original testing, 14 per cent (15 girls) were found to be delinquent; the rate of delinquency was twice as high among girls with invalidated profiles. However, it should be noted that the general rate among the girls is low.

Tables 1 and 2 show the distributions of these delinquents that had invalid profiles. It is not surprising that in comparison with youngsters who had valid profiles, for whom data are given in Tables 3 and 4, there seems to be a greater tendency for these delinquents to have started their misbehavior before (B group) testing. Also, among these delinquents the number of cases in the two more severe levels of misbehavior is several times that for level III. As will be shown below with reference to Tables 15 and 16, most of the children with invalid records who have a tendency toward delinquency obtained high F

TABLE 1. THE PERCENTAGES OF DELINQUENT BOYS AMONG ALL
THOSE WITH INVALID PROFILES THAT FALL INTO THE
VARIOUS CLASSES[a]

Time of Delinquent Act[b]	Levels of Delinquency				
	I	II	I & II	III	I, II, & III
A	2.5	8.7	11.2	5.0	16.2
B	5.0	11.8	16.8	3.1	19.9
C	.6	.6	1.2	0.0	1.2
B & C	5.6	12.4	18.0	3.1	21.1
A, B, & C	8.1	21.1	29.2	8.1	37.3

[a] Total boys with invalid profiles, 161; total delinquent among these, 60. To change the percentages to corresponding ones based on 60, multiply by 2.7.

[b] In this table and those following, A indicates after testing, B before testing, and C continuous.

TABLE 2. THE PERCENTAGES OF DELINQUENT GIRLS AMONG ALL
THOSE WITH INVALID PROFILES THAT FALL INTO THE
VARIOUS CLASSES[a]

Time of Delinquent Act	Levels of Delinquency				
	I	II	I & II	III	I, II, & III
A	1.9	3.8	5.7	0.0	5.7
B	1.9	1.9	3.8	2.9	6.7
A & B	3.8	5.7	9.5	2.9	12.4
Unclass.[b]	0.0	1.9	1.9	0.0	1.9
A, B, & Unclass.	3.8	7.6	11.4	2.9	14.3

[a] Total girls with invalid profiles, 105; total delinquent among these, 15. To change the percentages to corresponding ones based on 15, multiply by 7.0.

[b] These were 24 shoplifters who cannot be classified as A or B.

scores. Among probable sources of a high F in these cases is direct carelessness in answering, so that we could interpret these findings by saying that as an initial hypothesis boys and girls who under routine circumstances in the school setting answer so carelessly or understand so poorly the task presented to them as to obtain a high F score are prone to delinquency.

Tables 3 and 4 show the distributions of the delinquents with valid profiles by level and time of delinquency. These tables give the figures for the sum of classes I and II, the more definitely delinquent categories; and they also show the summed percentages for the B and C time categories, bringing these together because in both cases the testing occurred after some unsociable acts had been committed. In Table 2 it can be seen that approximately 14 per cent of all boys were placed in class I or II, the more severe categories. In other terms, more

TABLE 3. THE PERCENTAGES OF DELINQUENT BOYS AMONG ALL THOSE WITH VALID PROFILES THAT FALL INTO THE VARIOUS CLASSES[a]

Time of Delinquent Act	Levels of Delinquency				
	I	II	I & II	III	I, II, & III
A	.7	5.2	5.9	4.3	10.2
B	.8	5.3	6.1	2.4	8.5
C	.9	.9	1.8	0.0	1.8
B & C	1.7	6.2	7.9	2.4	10.3
A, B, & C	2.4	11.4	13.8	6.7	20.5

[a] Total boys with valid profiles, 1836; total delinquent among these, 376. To change the percentages to corresponding ones based on 376, multiply by 4.9.

TABLE 4. THE PERCENTAGES OF DELINQUENT GIRLS AMONG ALL THOSE WITH VALID PROFILES THAT FALL INTO THE VARIOUS CLASSES[a]

Time of Delinquent Act	Levels of Delinquency				
	I	II	I & II	III	I, II, & III
A	.7	2.1	2.8	.7	3.5
B	.3	1.0	1.3	1.1	2.4
A & B	1.0	3.1	4.1	1.8	5.9
Unclass.	0.0	1.2	1.2	0.0	1.2
A, B, & Unclass.	1.0	4.3	5.3	1.9	7.2

[a] Total girls with valid profiles, 1946; total delinquent among these, 140. To change the percentages to corresponding ones based on 140, multiply by 13.9.

than one in every eight of the ninth-grade sample had, by age 17, been involved in fairly severe misbehavior. The corresponding figure for the girls was about 5 per cent; thus the rate among girls is about one in twenty.

The reader should keep in mind that this particular follow-up depended only upon a check of the local records in establishing these percentages. Youths who had committed offenses in other counties or who had moved away and were lost to the study could not, at this time, be a part of the data. And, since the number of such unavailable cases is unknown, these percentages could not be corrected upward as they probably should be. The true percentages, which would be obtained by counting only those cases continuing in the city to obtain a denominator, should be somewhat higher. We feel confident, therefore, that within the meaning of the established categories, the percentages in the tables are minimal; they merely suggest the rates that are exemplary of the order produced by the data available.

Among all the girls of the study, only 1 per cent ended up in class I. No girl had behaved in a pattern so consistently unsocial as to be placed in the C class. More than 4 per cent of the girls had been involved in enough misbehavior to be classified either I or II. About 3 per cent of all girls both committed their offenses after the time of testing and received a classification of I or II. This percentage is derived from 54 girls.

The girls marked Unclassified in Table 4 are a group of girls about whom no definitive data were available beyond the fact that they had, at some time previous to the follow-up, been caught shoplifting. The records for juvenile shoplifters are, under special arrangement, intentionally restricted to mere registration of names by the police department; and classification of this subgroup of girls as A, B, or C was impossible. On the other hand, discussion with those who knew the type of case registered as shoplifter indicated their classification in the second category of severity of misbehavior. No girl was included in this group who had not certainly been stealing fairly important items in a store. There were 26 complete profiles on these girls, but 2 were invalid.

Tables 5 to 8 deal with the 376 delinquent boys and 116 delinquent girls (omitting the unclassified cases) who obtained valid MMPI profiles, and show the percentage of delinquents that were placed in the various levels of severity and in the different timing categories. For example, in Table 5, which has been calculated in order to show the percentage having the three different timing relationships, one may

TABLE 5. THE PERCENTAGES OF DELINQUENT BOYS AMONG THOSE
IN THE I, II, AND III SEVERITY LEVELS WHOSE OFFENSE TIMING
WAS A, B, AND C

Time of Delinquent Act	Levels of Delinquency				
	I, N = 43	II, N = 210	I & II, N = 253	III, N = 123	I, II, & III, N = 376
A	28	46	43	64	50
B	32	46	44	36	41
C	40	8	13	0	9
B & C	72	54	57	36	50

TABLE 6. THE PERCENTAGES OF DELINQUENT GIRLS AMONG THOSE
IN THE I, II, AND III SEVERITY LEVELS WHOSE OFFENSE TIMING
WAS A OR B[a]

Time of Delinquent Act	Levels of Delinquency				
	I, N = 20	II,[b] N = 60	I & II, N = 80	III, N = 36	I, II, & III, N = 116
A	70	67	68	39	59
B	30	33	32	61	41

[a] No girl was given a continuous rating.
[b] These cases do not include the Unclassified girls.

TABLE 7. THE PERCENTAGES OF DELINQUENT BOYS AMONG THOSE
IN THE A, B, AND C TIME CLASSES THAT WERE PLACED IN
EACH OF THE SEVERITY LEVELS OF OFFENSE

Levels of Delinquency	Time of Delinquent Act				
	A, N = 187	B, N = 155	C, N = 34	B & C, N = 189	A, B, & C, N = 376
I	6	9	50	16	11
II	51	63	50	60	56
I & II	57	72	100	76	67
III	42	28	0	23	33

TABLE 8. THE PERCENTAGES OF DELINQUENT GIRLS AMONG THOSE
IN THE A AND B TIME CLASSES THAT WERE PLACED IN
EACH OF THE SEVERITY LEVELS OF OFFENSE

Levels of Delinquency	Time of Delinquent Act		
	A, N = 68	B, N = 48	A & B, N = 116
I	21	12	17
II[a]	59	42	52
I & II	80	54	69
III	21	46	31

[a] These cases do not include the Unclassified girls.

see that 28 per cent of the delinquent boys with valid profiles committed offenses of the first level of severity after the time of testing. Similarly, 72 per cent of all the delinquent boys with valid profiles committed offenses of the first degree of severity either before the time of testing or both before and after testing. If one considers all three levels of offense severity together, then about 50 per cent committed their offenses after testing and the other 50 per cent started being offenders before the time of testing. In Table 6 similar percentages for the girls are given. In this case, none of the girls was given a C timing. Here, if all classes are considered together, 59 per cent of the girls committed their offenses after the time of testing.

Table 7 shows the percentages in each of the levels of offense severity; for most purposes we will combine levels I and II. In Table 7 it may be seen that levels I and II include 57 per cent of the 187 boys who committed offenses after the time of testing. Among the 155 boys who committed offenses before the time of testing, 72 per cent were placed in grades I or II. Table 8 gives similar figures for the girls. An almost identical percentage of the girls were placed in categories I and II as had been for the boys although more of the girls committed offenses after the time of testing. As a general indication from these tables about the best possible timing in making a predictive study, it would seem that the ninth grade was somewhat late, since a very considerable number of the children had already been in some sort of trouble. We had surmised that this might be the case and had chosen nevertheless to use the ninth grade because of the unproven assumption that the MMPI would not be well adapted to the eighth or seventh grades. It might be pointed out that this assumption is still not proven and in fact no evidence came out in the course of these studies that would indicate against using at least the eighth grade in any future surveys.

Tables 9 and 10 begin the presentation of the data indicating the relationship of these various delinquency levels and timings to the MMPI measurements. The general plan of presentation is to simplify the classes as much as possible in order to bring out more clearly whatever significant differences may in general exist. First, in Tables 9 through 14, we will present in the usual way statistics for the various individual scales. Following this we will attempt to show some of the relationships brought out by using the coded profile patterns.

In Table 9 the means on the various scales are given for the boys at each of the three levels of delinquency, and in both the after and before timing categories. Insofar as the differences between MMPI scale

TABLE 9. THE MEANS FOR BOYS AT THE THREE DELINQUENCY LEVELS

Scale	IA, N = 12	IIA, N = 96	IIIA, N = 79	Difference between: IA and IIA	Difference between: IIA and IIIA	IB, N = 14	IIB, N = 97	IIIB, N = 44	Difference between: IB and IIB	Difference between: IIB and IIIB
L	4.1	3.4	3.4	.7	0.0	4.1	3.7	3.6	.4	.1
F	6.6	7.1	6.3	−.5	.8	6.1	7.6	6.8	−1.5	.8
K	55.1	52.3	53.1	2.8	−.8	54.4	52.3	52.3	2.1	0.0
0 (Si)	46.1	50.5	51.1	−4.4	−.6	53.0	53.0	51.4	0.0	1.6
1 (Hs)	50.5	52.2	51.9	−1.7	.3	51.2	52.6	51.5	−1.4	1.1
2 (D)	45.0	49.2	50.7	−4.2	−1.5	53.1	52.9	51.2	.2	1.7
3 (Hy)	51.6	51.1	52.5	.5	−1.4	50.9	52.7	52.5	−1.8	.2
4 (Pd)	63.4	62.5	60.8	.9	1.7	67.1	65.7	64.9	1.4	.8
5 (Mf)	50.6	49.5	51.2	1.1	−1.7	48.5	50.6	51.8	−2.1	−1.2
6 (Pa)	55.8	52.4	52.9	3.4	−.5	49.8	56.0	54.5	−6.2**	1.5
7 (Pt)	53.8	55.9	56.5	−2.1	−.6	55.6	58.2	56.4	−2.6	1.8
8 (Sc)	64.2	60.3	60.8	3.9	−.5	58.3	64.3	60.3	−6.0**	4.0*
9 (Ma)	63.0	62.7	62.0	.3	.7	57.1	61.4	61.0	−4.3	.4

* Signifies a difference reliable above the 5 per cent level of confidence.
** Signifies a difference reliable above the 1 per cent level of confidence.

means are concerned, the three delinquency levels do not seem well differentiated. One would expect a decreasing mean Pd scale 4 in the progression from level I to level III. This occurs consistently in both the A and B groups, but the differences are not marked. No other set of differences is even this consistent. There are several statistically significant differences, but the lack of consistency of the over-all pattern makes it doubtful if any real reliance can be placed upon these. In general, the data of Table 9 are only weakly in support of the hypothesis that the differences between the three delinquency levels are closely related to MMPI scales. Unfortunately, the number of subjects in the first level of delinquency is so small that random factors possibly obscure what might otherwise be significant differences. On the other hand, it is possible that hypotheses could be evolved that would bring greater order into the observed differences. For example, scale 2, depression, shows a progressive decrease in average value from the IIIA group to the IA group. Similarly, there is a decrease among the B groups from I to III. The boys who committed their offenses after testing have very low depression scores, whereas those who had already committed some offenses have a depression average that is slightly greater as the offense severity is greater.

In Table 10 similar data are presented for the delinquent girls. Because of the small numbers involved, levels I and II have been combined. Even with this combination the number of girls for the comparison remains very small. Among the girls of these samples, the A

TABLE 10. THE MEANS FOR GIRLS OF COMBINED DELINQUENCY LEVELS I AND II AND LEVEL III

Scale	IA & IIA, N = 54	IIIA, N = 14	Difference between IA & IIA and IIIA	IB & IIB, N = 26	IIIB, N = 22	Difference between IB & IIB and IIIB
L	3.2	2.9	.3	2.9	3.5	—.6
F	7.3	6.5	.8	7.3	6.5	.8
K	50.4	52.1	—1.7	48.6	47.8	.8
0 (Si)	53.5	52.6	.9	56.4	56.2	.2
1 (Hs) ...	47.6	48.7	—1.1	46.7	47.1	—.4
2 (D)	48.1	50.3	—2.2	49.5	48.9	.6
3 (Hy) ...	50.0	53.5	—3.5	50.8	48.8	2.0
4 (Pd) ...	64.7	64.6	.1	68.5	61.1	7.4
5 (Mf) ...	55.6	52.4	3.2	60.8	57.5	3.3
6 (Pa) ...	54.3	53.1	1.2	56.9	57.0	—.1
7 (Pt) ...	55.4	54.7	.7	54.0	52.1	1.9
8 (Sc) ...	60.9	60.9	0.0	62.1	59.6	2.5
9 (Ma)...	62.3	58.3	4.0	60.0	59.8	.2

groups show no difference on scale 4 although there is a fairly large but unreliable difference between the B groups. The D scale again behaves as it did for the boys but the differences are not significant. In fact, perhaps because of the small N's, none of the differences of Table 10 is reliable.

TABLE 11. THE MEANS FOR DELINQUENT BOYS OF THE IA & IIA AND IBC & IIBC COMBINED GROUPS COMPARED TO THE CONTROL GROUP

				Difference between:		
Scale	IA & IIA,[a] N = 108	IBC & IIBC,[b] N = 145	Control,[c] N = 200	IA & IIA and IBC & IIBC	IA & IIA and Control	IBC & IIBC and Control
L	3.5	3.7	3.7	—.2	—.2	0.0
F	7.0	7.2	5.7	—.2	1.3 **	1.5 **
K	52.6	52.9	53.8	—.3	—1.2	—.9
0 (Si)	50.1	52.4	51.9	—2.3 *	—1.8 *	.5
1 (Hs)	52.1	52.2	51.7	—.1	.4	.5
2 (D)	48.8	52.2	52.1	—3.4 **	—3.3 **	.1
3 (Hy)	51.2	52.4	51.7	—1.2	—.5	.7
4 (Pd)	62.6	65.8	58.4	—3.2 **	4.2 **	7.4 **
5 (Mf)	49.6	50.0	52.8	—.4	—3.2 **	—2.8 *
6 (Pa)	52.8	54.9	52.0	—2.1 *	.8	2.9 **
7 (Pt)	55.7	57.9	56.9	—2.2	—1.2	1.0
8 (Sc)	60.7	62.7	58.6	—2.0	2.1	4.1 **
9 (Ma)	62.7	61.1	58.0	1.6	4.7 **	3.1 **

* Signifies a difference reliable above the 5 per cent level of confidence.
** Signifies a difference reliable above the 1 per cent level of confidence.
[a] Code, '4987-.
[b] Code, '4897-.
[c] Code, '8947-.

Tables 11 through 14 contrast average MMPI data for the delinquents with the data for a control group; but, before developing the findings of Table 11 and those following, it is necessary to describe the control group used. In order to obtain a basic sample with relatively smaller numbers of cases for correlation and other comparative studies, two correlation groups, one of 200 boys and one of 200 girls, were chosen. These groups, used in the earlier analysis of the characteristics of all ninth-graders, were selected to be representative samples. As a control in presentation of the delinquent data, they were modified somewhat by taking out of each group every child who showed any available evidence of delinquency. Each case taken out was replaced by another chosen from the same school and in a random fashion. Therefore the control groups of boys and girls as used in the tables dealing with delinquency overlap in large part with the correlation

TABLE 12. THE MEANS FOR DELINQUENT GIRLS OF THE IA & IIA, IB & IIB, AND UNCLASSIFIED II GROUPS COMPARED TO THE CONTROL GROUP

Scale	IA & IIA,[a] N = 54	IB & IIB,[b] N = 26	Unclass. II,[c] N = 24	Control,[d] N = 200	Difference between:			
					IA & IIA and IB & IIB	IA & IIA and Control	IB & IIB and Control	Unclass. II and Control
L	3.2	2.9	2.8	3.9	.3	−.7*	−1.0*	−1.1**
F	7.3	7.3	6.0	4.8	0.0	2.5**	2.5**	1.2*
K	50.4	48.6	52.2	54.0	1.8	−3.6**	−5.4**	−1.8
0 (Si)	53.5	56.4	50.9	52.9	−2.9	.6	3.5*	−2.0
1 (Hs)	47.6	46.7	46.9	47.9	.9	−.3	−1.2	−1.0
2 (D)	48.1	49.5	44.6	47.9	−1.4	.2	1.6*	−3.3**
3 (Hy)	50.0	50.8	50.6	50.8	−.8	−.8	0.0	−.2
4 (Pd)	64.7	68.5	62.4	58.4	−3.8	6.3**	10.1**	4.0**
5 (Mf)	55.6	60.8	54.8	54.9	−5.2*	.7	5.9**	−.1
6 (Pa)	54.3	56.9	56.2	52.5	−2.6	1.8	4.4**	3.7**
7 (Pt)	55.4	54.0	52.9	54.2	1.4	1.2	−.2	−1.3
8 (Sc)	60.9	62.1	57.2	56.3	−1.2	4.6**	5.8**	.9
9 (Ma)	62.3	60.0	61.6	56.0	2.3	6.3**	4.0**	5.6**

* Signifies a difference reliable above the 5 per cent level of confidence.
** Signifies a difference reliable above the 1 per cent level of confidence.
[a] Code, '49857-.
[b] Code, '485906-.
[c] Code, '49 865-2.
[d] Code, '489-.

groups described earlier but differ in that all cases of known delinquency, in any degree, have been replaced with cases without such a
history. The overlap of identical cases was 80 per cent of the boys and
83 per cent of the girls. Undoubtedly these control groups still have a
few delinquent cases in them and undoubtedly some of the children in
these control groups will, by the time of a later follow-up, have become
delinquent. For the present we can merely accept them as typical of
the whole sample except for the selection avoiding known delinquency
cases.

Except for a smaller scale 4 mean, the changes in the means of this
nondelinquent control group contrasted to those of the unselected
correlation group are relatively insignificant. The increase in the mean
for scale 4 amounts to only about one T score point. This change is
small, but it becomes fairly important when one considers the amount
of overlap among the numbers of the two groups and also when one
considers that one point represents a large proportion of the observed
differences between the control means and the means of the delinquent samples.

Both Tables 11 and 12, comparing delinquents of levels I and II
with the control group, show a fairly consistent tendency for the BC
group to be more maladjusted than the A group. The most significant
trend is of course on scale 4. The boys who committed their offenses
after the time of testing also show a lower depression. In fact this
depression score on scale 2 for the A group is below the adult normal
average. The absence of depression relates to the incidence of delinquency and to the timing of it. Both boy and girl A samples obtain
higher mean scores on Ma. This finding, consistent with the lower D,
further emphasizes the carefree character of the youngsters who had
not committed antisocial acts before testing. Both boys and girls who
had committed such acts before testing tend to obtain slightly higher
scale 6 scores, which may be related to the fact that they were in
reality under more surveillance and expressed somewhat appropriate
feelings of being controlled or limited by others. Particularly among
the girls there was also a tendency for the B group to have less defensiveness in admission of adverse facts about themselves as indicated by L and K; this might also be described as better insight into
their faults and peculiarities.

The A and BC groups differ in similar directions from the control
groups although there are differences in amount. In general, the A
delinquents are a little more like the control samples.

Table 11 permits specific comparisons of the boys judged to be in the two more severe classes of delinquency with the male control group. The F score was higher for both the A and BC boys than for the control boys. Corresponding to this, in the A group at any rate, there was a slightly lower L score. Also, in the same direction, there was a lower K for both the A and BC groups. Among these validity score differences the F differences were the only ones that were statistically reliable.

As has been found in the research of others on the relationship of the various MMPI scales to delinquency, Table 11 shows a significant and reliable difference for scale 4. This average difference is larger for those boys who had already committed asocial acts, the BC group, than for the group who got into trouble after testing.

Scale 5 shows the control group with a reliably larger mean score on both comparisons. These differences indicate a more nearly adult average level of masculinity for the delinquent boys, with the control boys more feminine than the average adult. There is also a reliable and significant difference on scale 6, which would mean a greater sensitivity and feeling of being controlled on the part of the BC group. This is consistent with the fact, as stated above, that many of these boys were marked in their communities and certainly were conscious of the fact that they were known to the court or police. Both delinquent groups of boys obtained higher scale 8 mean scores than did the control. This suggests that a considerable number of these boys have the characteristics of schizoid persons. The control mean for this scale is already larger than that of the average adult. The same point applies in approximately equal degree to the means for scale 9 where, as is usual for adolescents, the control group mean is already high but not so high that the two groups of delinquents fail to go higher. In this a significant number of delinquents are similar to the manic adult patient.

Table 12 shows comparative data on girls at levels I and II. In contrast to the boys, there were no C type ratings for the girls. Separate data are included on the shoplifting group of 24 girls called Unclassified II cases because, although their offenses were rated as being comparable to the second level of delinquency, the timing could not be used to subdivide them into A and B groups.

The differences between the A and B groups of girls are similar to those observed among the boys. The B group has a slightly higher Pd, scale 4. This group also shows a higher scale 6 mean, and the A group is a little higher on scale 9. In addition to these trends, the B girls show a higher scale 5 mean score indicating greater masculinity in contrast to those of the A group. The Unclassified II shoplifting girls present some interesting contrasts with the other groups. They are, on some scales, between the B group and the control group in their deviations; but they are more extroverted than the other delinquents as indicated by scale 0, and they obtain the lowest mean depression score and the lowest mean Pt of any of the four samples.

When we compare these three groups of delinquent girls and the control group, again scale 4 shows the most consistent differentiation; but a number of other scales also show significant and reliable differences. The tendency noted among the delinquent boys to obtain higher F scores is even more marked in delinquent girls. Similarly, the delinquent girls obtain lower K scores. Although higher F scores in delinquents might be attributed to carelessness, the same factor could not explain the low K score. It is simpler to assume that both derive from test-taking attitude, with the delinquents more like average adults; the nondelinquent controls deviate toward defensive answers.

Particularly in the case of the girls, the presence of the factor of control or guardedness as measured by K lessens the likelihood of delinquency. This is consistent with our general clinical impression that, as patients get better from psychoneurotic illness, their K scores rise.

The mean score for the control group girls on scale 5 shows some tendency to masculinity of interests, but this trend is even greater for the A and B delinquent groups. As was true with the boys, the scores on scale 6 are larger among B delinquents and here again this could be explained by the fact that some of them were on probation. As with the delinquent boys, scales 8 and 9 are very high for delinquent girls. Again this means that the schizoid and manic personality patterns are prominent.

In general summary, the findings in Tables 11 and 12 show that scales 4, 8, and 9 are consistent in indicating that many delinquent adolescents respond to MMPI items like the adult clinical cases that were used to derive these scales. In more technical terms, these trends could be described as less concern with the consequences of asocial acts, more active and uninhibited social contacts, and bizarre or distorted semantic content. There is also a moderate tendency in boys and a stronger one in girls toward "plus getting" (MMPI jargon denoting a person who emphasizes his psychological defects; it is associated with high F scores). Neurotic traits do not seem to be marked in any groups, delinquent or normal. By contrast, the delinquent groups, particularly those who became delinquent after the time of

| | | | | Difference between: | |
Scale	IIIA,[a] N = 79	IIIB,[b] N = 44	Control,[c] N = 200	IIIA and Control	IIIB and Control
L	3.4	3.6	3.7	—.3	—.1
F	6.3	6.8	5.7	.6	1.1
K	53.1	52.3	53.8	—.7	—1.5
0 (Si)	51.1	51.4	51.9	—.8	—.5
1 (Hs)	51.9	51.5	51.7	.2	—.2
2 (D)	50.7	51.2	52.1	—1.4	—.9
3 (Hy)	52.5	52.5	51.7	.8	.8
4 (Pd)	60.8	64.9	58.4	2.4	6.5 **
5 (Mf)	51.2	51.8	52.8	—1.6	—1.0
6 (Pa)	52.9	54.5	52.0	.9	2.5
7 (Pt)	56.5	56.4	56.9	—.4	—.5
8 (Sc)	60.8	60.3	58.6	2.2	1.7
9 (Ma)	62.0	61.0	58.0	4.0 *	3.0

* Signifies a difference reliable above the 5 per cent level of confidence.
** Signifies a difference reliable above the 1 per cent level of confidence.
[a] Code, '9487–.
[b] Code, '4987–.
[c] Code, '8947–.

| | | | | Difference between: | |
Scale	IIIA,[a] N = 14	IIIB,[b] N = 22	Control,[c] N = 200	IIIA and Control	IIIB and Control
L	2.9	3.5	3.9	—1.0	—.4
F	6.5	6.5	4.8	1.7	1.7 *
K	52.1	47.8	54.0	—1.9	—6.2 **
0 (Si)	52.6	56.2	52.9	—.3	3.3 **
1 (Hs)	48.7	47.1	47.9	.8	—.8
2 (D)	50.3	48.9	47.9	2.4	1.0
3 (Hy)	53.5	48.8	50.8	2.7	—2.0
4 (Pd)	64.6	61.1	58.4	6.2	2.7
5 (Mf)	52.4	57.5	54.9	—2.5	2.6
6 (Pa)	53.1	57.0	52.5	—.6	4.5
7 (Pt)	54.7	52.1	54.2	.5	—2.1
8 (Sc)	60.9	59.6	56.3	4.6	3.3
9 (Ma)	58.3	59.8	56.0	2.3	3.8

* Signifies a difference reliable above the 5 per cent level of confidence.
** Signifies a difference reliable above the 1 per cent level of confidence.
[a] Code, '4897–.
[b] Code, '498 560–.
[c] Code, '489–.

testing, show the least depression and, among girls, obtain average standard scores even smaller than the normal adult.

Data in Tables 13 and 14 are similar to those in Tables 11 and 12 except that the presumptively milder class III delinquents are compared with the control cases. Although the numbers of cases are for the most part too small for reliable differences to show up readily, the general trend of differences bears out the findings of Tables 11 and 12. The findings also reinforce the indications of Tables 9 and 10 that the children whose names appear on the police register, even though the offenses are seemingly minor, are more like those who appear in major categories of delinquency than they are like the control cases who are without recorded delinquency.

Table 15 presents a most important outcome of the research. In it are indicated preliminary probabilities for delinquency when one starts with a given code simplified to the highest two T scores on the profiles. The code frequencies of Table 15 were obtained by classifying the codes as described for similar data in the *Atlas for the Clinical Use of the MMPI* (37). Codes with no underlining in the first two scale symbols are simply classed by those symbols. If the second and other symbols are underlined, the class is similarly determined by the first two. If the first two symbols alone are underlined, the code is classed as one half in each order of the two symbols. (This accounts for the .5 frequencies of the table.) Finally, codes with underlining that goes beyond the first two symbols were classed as indeterminate (Indet.).

The table lists the actual frequencies of codes for all the ninth-graders together with the percentages that became delinquent corresponding to each of these. For example, one may read that among the 45 boys of the total sample who received no score greater than 54 (code class –), only 9 per cent were or became delinquent. Of the 43 girls in this code class none was delinquent. At the end of the table one finds that the over-all percentage of delinquency for boys is 22 and for girls 8. The percentages of delinquency for profiles when the highest scale is at least as large as T score 70 are larger and those for the less elevated profiles lower, showing a preponderant positive relation between profile height and delinquency rates.

Individual statistics are more interesting, however. In each category the effect of the profile type on the delinquency rate can be judged by comparing its rate to the over-all rate in the given column. For example, there were 85 boy and 73.5 girl profiles having a high code beginning with 49; of the former 38 per cent and of the latter 16 per cent

TABLE 15. THE PERCENTAGES OF CHILDREN IN THE DIFFERENT CODE CLASSES WHO BECAME DELINQUENT

Code Class	Boys						Girls					
	Number in Profile Type			Per Cent Delinquent			Number in Profile Type			Per Cent Delinquent		
	<70	≥70	Total	<70	≥70	Total	<70	≥70	Total	<70	≥70	Total
L > 9			50			20			42			5
F > 15			103			49			58			22
? invalid			8			0			5			0
Indet.	98	10	108	15	60	19	108	12	120	7	25	9
–	45	0	45	9	0	9	43	0	43	0	0	0
0–	18	2	20	0	0	0	34	0	34	0	0	0
01	2	0.5	2.5	50	0	40	1	3	4	0	0	0
02	19.5	4	23.5	21	25	21	16.5	5	21.5	3	0	2
03	4	0	4	0	0	0	4	1	5	0	0	0
04	13	0	13	15	0	15	31	8.5	39.5	5	0	4
05	4	1	5	50	0	40	41.5	1	42.5	7	100	9
06	4.5	1.5	6	0	67	17	25	5	30	0	0	0
07	12.5	3	15.5	16	0	13	21.5	8	29.5	14	0	10
08	9.5	2.5	12	0	40	8	17.5	6	23.5	14	0	11
09	6	0	6	0	0	0	14	2	16	0	0	0
Total 0	93	14.5	107.5	12	21	13	206	39.5	245.5	5	3	5
1–	2	0	2	50	0	50	0	0	0	0	0	0
10	2	1.5	3.5	50	0	29	0	1	1	0	0	0
12	3.5	1	4.5	14	50	22	0	0	1	0	0	0
13	5	5.5	10.5	0	27	14	2.5	2	4.5	0	50	22
14	7	3	10	36	30	35	1	0	1	0	0	0
15	1	2	3	0	0	0	0	0	0	0	0	0
16	1.5	1.5	3	0	0	0	0	0	0	0	0	0
17	2.5	6	8.5	0	0	0	0.5	0	0.5	0	0	0
18	3.5	7.5	11	0	0	0	1	1.5	1.5	0	0	0
19	2	1	3	0	0	0	1	0	1	0	0	0
Total 1	30	29	59	17	10	14	6	4.5	10.5	0	22	10

TABLE 15 continued

Code Class	Boys						Girls					
	Number in Profile Type			Per Cent Delinquent			Number in Profile Type			Per Cent Delinquent		
	<70	≥70	Total	<70	≥70	Total	<70	≥70	Total	<70	≥70	Total
2-	14	0	14	14	0	14	1	0	1	0	0	0
20	8.5	6	14.5	12	33	21	1.5	0	1.5	33	0	33
21	2.5	3	5.5	20	17	18	0	0	0	0	0	0
23	2.5	4	6.5	20	0	8	2.5	1.5	2.5	0	0	0
24	7.5	7	14.5	20	0	10	2.5	0	4	0	0	0
25	3.5	2	5.5	0	0	0	0	0.5	0	0	0	0
26	0	0	0	0	0	0	2	0.5	2.5	0	0	0
27	6	3.5	9.5	17	14	16	0	2	0.5	0	0	0
28	4	3	7	0	0	0	2	0	2	0	0	0
29	1.5	1	2.5	0	0	12	1.5	4.5	1.5	5	0	3
Total 2	50	29.5	79.5	13	10	12	11	4.5	15.5	0	0	3
3-	10	0	10	20	0	20	9	0	9	0	0	0
30	0	0	0	0	0	0	3	0	3	0	0	0
31	7	3.5	10.5	14	43	24	2.5	3	5.5	0	0	0
32	2.5	0	2.5	60	0	60	0.5	0	0.5	0	0	0
34	10	2	12	30	25	29	14.5	5.5	20	0	0	0
35	6.5	0.5	7	23	0	21	4.5	0	4.5	0	0	0
36	1	0	1	0	0	0	4	1	5	0	0	0
37	2	0	2	0	0	0	2.5	0	2.5	0	0	0
38	2	1	3	25	0	17	2	0	2	0	0	0
39	2.5	0	2.5	0	0	0	3.5	1	4.5	0	0	0
Total 3	43.5	7	50.5	22	29	23	46	10.5	56.5	0	0	0
4-	17	3	20	24	67	30	25	1	26	16	22	17
40	12	4	16	25	25	25	16	4.5	20.5	0	0	0
41	11	8	19	5	38	18	1	2	3	0	0	5
42	18.5	18	36.5	8	17	12	11.5	7.5	19	7	13	14
43	23	8	31	22	56	31	13.5	7.5	21	3	27	6
45	15	6	21	13	50	24	45	14.5	59.5	3	14	16
46	20	17	37	18	29	23	27	28	55	6	27	16
47	21	24.5	45.5	17	24	21	23	10.5	33.5	13	0	9
48	42	58	100	24	35	31	29.5	41	70.5	5	27	18
49	45	40	85	27	51	38	40.5	33	73.5	7	26	16
Total 4	224.5	186.5	411	20	37	28	232	149.5	381.5	6	22	12

TABLE 15 continued

Code Class	Boys						Girls					
	Number in Profile Type			Per Cent Delinquent			Number in Profile Type			Per Cent Delinquent		
	<70	≥70	Total	<70	≥70	Total	<70	≥70	Total	<70	≥70	Total
5–	12	0	12	0	0	0	51	12	63	2	17	5
50	4	3	7	0	0	0	36.5	10	46.5	0	0	0
51	3	2	5	0	0	0	2	0	2	0	0	0
52	6.5	2	8.5	0	0	0	2	3	5	0	0	0
53	8.5	2.5	11	18	0	14	14.5	4	18.5	7	0	5
54	11	4	15	18	0	13	60	24.5	84.5	9	4	8
56	3.5	1	4.5	0	0	0	17	8	25	0	0	0
57	8.5	2	10.5	12	0	10	13	2.5	15.5	0	0	0
58	5	6	11	20	33	27	20.5	7.5	28	2	0	2
59	15.5	2.5	18	13	0	11	36.5	21	57.5	10	12	10
Total 5	77.5	25	102.5	10	8	9	253	92.5	345.5	5	6	5
6–	7	0	7	14	0	14	14	0	14	5	0	0
60	2.5	1.5	4	40	0	25	11	4	15	9	25	13
61	1.5	0.5	2	67	0	50	1	1	2	0	0	0
62	3	2	5	33	50	40	1	0.5	1.5	0	0	0
63	3	0	3	0	0	0	7	1	8	0	0	0
64	5	4	9	30	50	39	20	11	31	8	14	10
65	4.5	1	5.5	0	0	0	15	1	16	0	0	0
67	1.5	2.5	4	0	40	25	5	5.5	10.5	0	0	0
68	3	4.5	7.5	33	33	33	9.5	8	17.5	5	0	3
69	7.5	4.5	12	27	22	25	13.5	7.5	21	7	13	10
Total 6	38.5	20.5	59	22	32	25	97	39.5	136.5	4	9	5
7–	2	0	2	0	0	0	6	0	6	0	0	0
70	8.5	8	16.5	35	13	24	8.5	7	15.5	12	0	6
71	2.5	6	8.5	0	50	35	0.5	0	.5	0	0	0
72	1	7.5	8.5	0	20	18	5	1.5	6.5	0	0	0
73	3	2	5	0	0	0	5.5	1	6.5	0	0	0
74	11	12.5	23.5	14	16	15	7	1.5	8.5	0	0	0
75	2.5	0	2.5	0	0	0	7	1.5	8.5	28	0	24
76	1.5	3.5	5	0	0	0	3	3.5	6.5	0	0	0
78	10	24	34	30	19	22	14	5	19	4	0	3
79	5	4	9	20	25	22	6	1.5	7.5	0	0	0
Total 7	47	67.5	114.5	18	19	19	62.5	22.5	85	6	0	4

128

TABLE 15 continued

Code Class	Boys						Girls					
	Number in Profile Type			Per Cent Delinquent			Number in Profile Type			Per Cent Delinquent		
	<70	≥70	Total	<70	≥70	Total	<70	≥70	Total	<70	≥70	Total
8–	3	1	4	0	0	0	4	0	4	0	0	0
80	8.5	4.5	13	24	0	15	13.5	9	22.5	11	22	16
81	8.5	8.5	17	24	35	29	0	3.5	3.5	0	0	0
82	5	5	10	40	0	20	1	3	4	0	0	0
83	12	4	16	13	0	9	3	3	6	3	13	7
84	33	30	63	24	42	33	14.5	8	22.5	5	0	3
85	4	9	13	0	0	0	9.5	6.5	16	5	22	14
86	2	13.5	15.5	0	33	29	9.5	9	18.5	4	6	5
87	13	49	62	31	15	19	14	16	30	8	11	10
89	26.5	39	65.5	11	27	21	12.5	17.5	30	6	11	8
Total 8	115.5	163.5	279	19	23	22	81.5	75.5	157	4	0	4
9–	39	10	49	18	20	18	26	2	28	10	0	6
90	13	8	21	15	25	19	10	6	16	0	0	0
91	4	0	4	25	0	25	0	1	1	40	0	4
92	10.5	2	12.5	0	33	0	2.5	0	2.5	11	100	19
93	5.5	3	8.5	18	38	24	9.5	1	10.5	11	10	9
94	47	86	133	21	6	32	42.5	58	100.5	9	11	11
95	17.5	15.5	33	17	15	12	50.5	22	72.5	11	12	5
96	12.5	13.5	26	16	15	15	13.5	8.5	22	0	0	0
97	12	11	23	8	9	9	16	8.5	24.5	7	7	7
98	42.5	68	110.5	9	32	23	29.5	42.5	72	8	9	8
Total 9	203.5	217	420.5	15	29	22	200	149.5	349.5	8	9	8
Total	1066	770	1997	16	27	22	1346	600	2051	5	11	8

129

were or became delinquent. These rates compared to the corresponding over-all rates are respectively 68 and 100 per cent larger. Also, there were 40 boys and 33 girls whose score on scale 4 (at least) was greater than 69. For these two groups the delinquency rates were 51 and 26. It is clear that a profile coded 49 is highly indicative of delinquency and this indication is even stronger if the profile in question has its highest T score greater than or equal to 70. As a contrast to the profiles of type 49, note the figures for profile type 59. There were 18 boys who had this profile type, of whom only 11 per cent were delinquent. This rate is only 50 per cent of the over-all rate of delinquency in spite of the fact that the score on scale 9 is second highest as it was among the 49 group. Many other examples of high and low rates can be found. In each case the actual number of profiles in a category is given so the reader may gain an estimate of the stability of the corresponding delinquency rate.

It is impossible to analyze the general findings adequately or even state them in a satisfactory way. The reader will have to use this table as a guide to his own syntheses or more practically as a method of obtaining an estimate of the probability of delinquency from a coded profile. The small numbers of cases obtaining certain profiles make the corresponding percentages obviously unreliable. It is difficult to know when these percentages become reliably restricted to a small enough range for useful guidance. It is unlikely that delinquency percentages based on profiles having frequencies of less than five cases can be used very reliably, and it would seem to us that there should be at least ten examples in the original sample.

There are about 100 primary code types in Table 15. The total profile frequencies of each of these is divided into subgroupings of profiles having at least the largest T score greater than or equal to 70 and those having this score less than 70. Even among the numbers for total frequency only about 50 per cent of the profiles had an original frequency of ten or greater. Increasing the sample size is an obvious need in this work although some profiles are so rare that one would never be able to get reliably large numbers.

Some of the outstanding frequencies are given in Tables 16 and 17 for boys and girls respectively. Most of the data have been taken from Table 15 and are indicative of some combinations.

Largest among all observed delinquency rates is that for boys with F score greater than 15. The boy who under the conditions of testing that prevailed when this study was made obtains a high F is likely to become delinquent with almost a one out of two probability. Clini-

TABLE 16. THE RELATIVE RATES OF OCCURENCE OF CERTAIN CODED HIGH POINTS AMONG ALL NINTH-GRADE BOYS COMPARED WITH THE RATES OF DELINQUENCY

Coded High Points	Percentage of 1997 Codes	Percentage Delinquent in Code Class	Percentage of 436 Delinquents in Code Class	Relative Rate
L > 9	2.5	20.0	2.3	.92
F > 15	5.2	48.5	11.5	2.21
−	2.3	8.9	.9	.39
0	5.4	13.0	3.2	.59
1	3.0	13.6	1.8	.60
2	4.0	11.9	2.2	.55
3	2.5	22.8	2.6	1.04
4	20.6	27.6	26.0	1.26
5	5.1	9.3	2.2	.43
6	3.0	25.4	3.4	1.13
7	5.7	18.8	4.9	.86
8	14.0	21.7	13.9	.99
9	21.1	22.4	21.6	1.02
94 + 49	10.9	34.4	17.2	1.58
49′ + 94′ [a]	6.3	42.1	12.2	1.94
4′ [a]	9.4	36.7	15.7	1.67
9′ [a]	10.9	29.0	14.4	1.32

[a] The prime indicates the place of the 70 T score level.

TABLE 17. THE RELATIVE RATES OF OCCURRENCE OF CERTAIN CODED HIGH POINTS AMONG ALL NINTH-GRADE GIRLS COMPARED WITH THE RATES OF DELINQUENCY

Coded High Points	Percentage of 2051 Codes	Percentage Delinquent in Code Class	Percentage of 155 Delinquents in Code Class	Relative Rate
L > 9	2.0	5.0	1.3	.65
F > 15	2.8	22.0	8.4	3.00
−	2.1	0.0	0.0	0.00
0	12.0	4.7	7.4	.62
1	.5	9.5	.6	1.20
2	.8	3.2	.3	.38
3	2.8	0.0	0.0	0.00
4	18.6	12.3	30.3	1.63
5	16.8	4.9	11.0	.65
6	6.7	5.5	4.8	.72
7	4.1	4.1	2.3	.56
8	7.7	8.0	8.1	1.05
9	17.0	8.2	18.4	1.08
94 + 49	8.5	12.1	13.5	1.59
49′ + 94′ [a]	4.4	15.4	9.0	2.05
4′ [a]	7.3	22.1	21.3	2.92
9′ [a]	7.3	8.7	8.4	1.15

[a] The prime indicates the place of the 70 T score level.

131

cians have long regarded the F score as a personality measurement in itself; and if no more complicated interpretation is made than that the individual acts carelessly when most of his fellows are conforming to the task required, then these findings are reasonable. These boys obtaining high F scores made up 11.5 per cent of all observed delinquents. Finally, the delinquency rate for high F scores within these observations is 2.21, which means that the probability of a high F among delinquent boys is more than twice the corresponding rate, 5.2, observed among boys in general. The general sample rate, of course, includes the delinquent ones.

As a contrasting example, the male profiles in which no high point is coded (codes starting with –), constitute 2.3 per cent of all observed male profiles. Only 8.9 per cent of these boys were classified delinquent; they made up only .9 per cent of the delinquent group and the relative rate was .39. Thus the indicated relative delinquency rate was less than one fifth of that for boys having a high F.

A few of the combinations of high points that provide relatively high ratios are also given, but still higher ratios can be found in Table 15. The over-all data of these tables indicate that it is more reliable to predict that certain boys or girls will not get into trouble than that others will do so. All these tables represent only a first approximation at cutting points for prediction and of course are open to the criticism that all levels of delinquency and all timing categories had to be lumped together in order to make the rates reliable enough to have any stability.

Before we proceed to a summary of the indications from the code patterns in Tables 15, 16, and 17, it may be desirable to consider some of the possible theoretical structures into which the data might fall. We do this not with any intent to establish a stable theory but merely for orientation. General inspection of the tables gives some support to the hypothesis that the strength of a given scale as indicated by its T score contributes to the probability of delinquency, either as a positive or negative factor—is either an excitatory or an inhibitory indication. Higher T scores on some scales are associated with a greater probability of delinquency and thus could be considered excitatory to delinquency probabilities roughly in proportion to the height of the score. Two of these positive excitatory scales representing coordinate high points of a profile might with appropriate weights be added together so as to afford a higher component probability figure. Other scales that have a negative effect on probabilities would also affect delinquency probabilities. A negative inhibitory scale associated with low delinquency rates would, in combination with a positive excitor scale, bring about a component probability of smaller size than would be observed if the former were a positive or neutral factor. The smallest of all probabilities should, according to this theory, occur with the combination of two inhibitory scales.

An alternative theoretical structure of greater complexity would assume that the excitatory or inhibitory effect of a scale would not be a consistent character of this scale. The scale might assume a positive or negative sign relative to delinquency probability in certain combinations of high points but change sign with other combinations. In such a case all relationships would tend to be complex and the simple combination pattern described above would fail to predict the observed figure from the combinations of high points. If this more complex theoretical structure were supported, then at least in early stages of statistical analysis there would seem to be little system or order among combinations of scale high points, so that one could not predict the delinquency probability associated with a new combination of high points from data about the scales in known combinations.

We do not yet feel justified in attempting to establish one of these or other theoretical structures on the basis of present data. The observed delinquency probabilities for many of the combinations of Table 15 are patently unreliable. In some of the discussion that follows, however, we shall use the positive and negative excitatory and inhibitory terms as a convenience without meaning to commit ourselves to their continued usage in future writing or discussion when more adequate data may be available.

In summary, it has seemed to us as we considered the influence of the ten clinical variables that clinical experience was again supported in indicating that scale 2 is an inhibitor with negative influence on the probability of delinquency. The reader should note the relative frequencies of the two columns and the sums of the two columns of Table 15 that show the change as a variable is less than or greater than T score 70. With the same variable, these percentages change upward as the score is larger (note scale 4); in others, the percentages change downward (note scale 2). It has been clinical practice to say of the psychopath or other person who has gotten into difficulty that if he can develop a high score on depression, he has a better prognosis. From the data of Table 15, it appears that combinations of scores where scale 2 is one of the high points tend to have lower delinquency rates. This supports very nicely the clinical impression.

Scale 5 also seems to be negatively related to the occurrence of

delinquency in the boys. The frequency is low when 5 is the high
point and also in most combinations with 5. Only scale 4 is clearly
able to combine with 5 to produce a high rate. Again this seems in
accord with our clinical impressions. The trend is not so certain for
girls. Among boys, and less certainly among girls, scale 7 is also an
inhibitor relative to delinquent behavior.

Contrasting strongly with these inhibiting factors is the very strongly excitatory scale 4. This has been stressed above as the one scale
most likely to be indicative of delinquency in that it was derived from
clinical cases who were themselves, more often than not, young people
who had gotten into fairly serious trouble through asocial or amoral
acts. In the severe clinical case where one may speak of a formal
diagnostic category, psychopathic personality, these individuals commit asocial or amoral acts without apparent motivation and without
apparent ability to govern themselves or learn from experience. No
clinician would hold that these persons are the sole type committing
delinquent acts. No a priori reason should therefore exist to expect
that all delinquents would score high on this scale even if it were a
completely valid indicator of the category. On the other hand, nearly
any clinician assumes that the general characteristics of the severe
clinical class exist in minor degree among a great many young people
and also that many relatively severe cases of psychopathic personality
are handled by penal institutions and similar agencies. Because of this
assumed frequency of the syndrome, one should expect that scale 4
would be a very frequent indicator of delinquency, the positive trend
being canceled only when an inhibitory scale such as 2 is strong as
well. In any case, it would seem desirable to recognize and treat differently those delinquents in whom a scale 4 syndrome is dominant
over other factors.

Another general line of behavior disturbance that may be related
to delinquency is broadly characterized as psychosis, which, in the
adult person to whom the psychiatric terminology would be applied,
is a general term for severe mental illness. The most pertinent indicators of this pattern among the clinical scales of the MMPI are probably scales 6, 8, and 9; at least these scales are indicators of the com-
monest juvenile psychosis, schizophrenia, and also of the fairly common patterns of hypomania. It may be that prepsychotic and generally deviant schizoid youngsters are prone to asocial or amoral acts. If
so, these scales should show a tendency to elevation among delinquent
youths.

Tables 15, 16, and 17 do not permit easy interpretation of the three scales as either clearly positive or negative. However, combinations with them such as 86, 49, 84, and 94 seem to indicate a positive relation to delinquency. In contrast, 83, 85, 95, and 97 rather point to a negative influence. If such inconsistent indications persist with more reliable data, we may have evidence that would require more complex theory than would do for a finding that assigns a consistently positive or negative sign to a scale to show its effect on a combination. One thing is clear, however, in summary of the occurrence of profiles having psychotic shapes: many delinquent adolescents have profiles that are closely similar to those of adult psychotic patients.

Few delinquent (or nondelinquent) juveniles have neurotic profiles, but occasional ones occur and the persons obtaining them should certainly be recognized and separately treated.

In conclusion, we must repeat that the prediction rates presented here are in preliminary form and merely give an idea of the order of size rather than a final estimate. With modifications of coding and with better pattern analysis methodology, it seems reasonable to expect that prediction tables can be constructed having better ratios than are indicated here.

Significance of Findings

THE FOREGOING papers have demonstrated beyond reasonable question that some of the patterns of symptoms seen in adult mentally ill patients are more common among juvenile delinquents than chance would suggest. It has also become contrastingly apparent that others among the personality adjustment patterns of adults are observed less frequently than would be likely by chance among adolescent delinquents.

(These findings are, of course, contingent upon the assumption that MMPI patterns are valid indicators of the chief syndromes of adult maladjustment. The validity required to justify this assumption does not have to be high, but the fact that this assumption intervenes in our statements must be emphasized.)

The summary result is that the MMPI seems to provide useful categories into which a substantial number of delinquent adolescents will fall. These categories yield practical actuarial data that will provide basic expectation figures predicting relatively high and relatively low delinquency rates. It has also become apparent that a large proportion of delinquent adolescents do not show definite characteristics as measured by this instrument that would link them to known patterns of illness.

The outstanding finding in positive relationship between recognized scale meanings and delinquency is that the MMPI scales 4 and 9 have an excitatory role in the actuarial numbers predicting the development of asocial behavior. The results on these scales lead one toward the conclusion that the asocial, amoral psychopath and the hypomanic among the patterns of adult maladjustment are those chiefly represented among the adolescents. As inhibitors to delinquency probability, the neurotic adult patterns appear most definite. Depression, introversion, and femininity of interest pattern predicate possible relationships with the introvertive, self-critical, generally inhibited adult.

136

We can at present make no useful assertions about those other adolescent delinquents who exhibit deviant patterns within the categorical structure provided by the MMPI but whose delinquency rates are not different from the over-all expectation. It seems to us that this group is now more clearly defined and can in the future be isolated for special analysis and consideration as well as for the development of different approaches in understanding them and in deriving probability numbers for predictive purposes.

Also, those adolescents whose MMPI profiles show no high deviation, and who are thus indicated to be normal, are very unlikely to be found delinquent, and this finding seems to us to be more clearly substantiated in the data than is any positive probability trend.

In regard to treatment and general handling of delinquents, we feel very strongly that those who have the most clearly deviant patterns related to a high delinquency rate should be treated in a way more nearly than in present practice consistent with the approaches we have for adults who are recognized as being in need of professional psychological skills for the planning of their rehabilitation. It is true that no specific or even generally validated treatment approaches are available for these persons, but clinical practice has developed a considerable body of knowledge about the course of the familiar disorders and there are at least fairly well accepted practices suggesting the best ways of handling them. We would recommend for such individuals, therefore, professional advice and guidance supplementing the processes of law.

For those delinquents not classifiable at present either as delinquency-prone with deviant personality or as relatively not prone toward delinquency, no new recommendations appear to be indicated by these findings. One subclass among such youths may be persons who are not particularly prone to delinquency but who, through unusual force of circumstances, have been embroiled in a series of acts that have led to their being delinquent. If this hypothesis is substantiated, one would expect that such cases would be distinguished by the rarity with which they repeat their acts and they could be handled accordingly. Identification of such an individual beyond the test findings would probably rest upon careful evaluation of the circumstances leading to the antisocial behavior; such study would probably show the relatively inactive part played by the individual in question. Since this kind of investigation is routine in connection with better courts and probation offices, the recommendation would amount to suggesting that such individuals be given more attention, and also that such investigatory facilities be expanded at least for these persons.

Apart from considerations about the nature and handling of the delinquent, we feel that these findings have been most encouraging in the relationship they show between groups having certain of the MMPI profile patterns and high or low probability for the occurrence of delinquency.

There are few clinicians who do not believe firmly in the validity of their "hunches" based on experience, hunches in which they feel strongly that a given case will or will not do well on parole or probation. But experimental study of these predictive hunches has shown them to be unreliable. In any case, there is a very considerable need for improved objective figures so that reproducible classification can provide data on which parole, probation, and treatment agencies can judge the effectiveness of their rehabilitation programs. This need for objective prediction devices is equally imperative for evaluating the activities of preventive agencies where an attempt is made to provide programs that should decrease the delinquency rate among participants. For all such applications, the probability figures provided here should offer a guide. If, by some program of supervision or treatment, the rate of delinquency among a defined subgroup of adolescents can be cut beyond the probable error, then we may feel that we have established, perhaps for the first time scientifically, the validity of such a program.

We believe also that these findings have exceedingly great value in providing objective indications for isolating groups of adolescents who are very unlikely to get into serious trouble. This prediction seems to be a more stable one than the positive prediction of delinquency itself. The identification of boys and girls who are relatively unlikely to become delinquent should permit us to relax our efforts, usually negative, to combat probable misbehavior among *all* adolescents; we should, by eliminating those unlikely to get into trouble, be able to work more constructively with the smaller group that remains.

We come finally to consideration of the practical use of the MMPI or similar instruments in the schools or in other legitimate agencies. MMPI profiles are objectively obtained, and the classes of profile and basic data for interpretation as these are discussed in the foregoing papers are all reproducible from clinic to clinic with little difficulty. It cannot be too strongly emphasized, however, that the MMPI cannot be objectively used without adequate preparation of the responsible clinician. We would emphasize first of all the need for this caution in the procedure of administration, where the test-taking attitude on the part of those being evaluated by the Inventory can be so important as to determine over a wide range the validities of the profiles.

This caution also applies with force to the interpretation of the data once they have been obtained; we are concerned that probability figures such as those given here shall be clearly evaluated and cautiously applied in particular situations. The use of a probability figure is itself something that requires training and broad understanding of the meaning of such statistics. For example, we could choose a group of boys who had, according to the presumptive probabilities from these papers, a 45 per cent probability of becoming delinquent. One who is to use such a figure must understand its group meaning. He cannot say that any given boy has such a probability; he is not by any means safe in saying that this probability is identical with the final delinquency rate that would be observed for the group. All prediction figures have error allowance and they all operate under the assumption that new samples to which they are applied are similar to the derivative ones and that conditions of testing and the like are reasonably identical. It is not possible to calculate the error allowance, but the experienced clinician tends to develop some understanding of its limits as they may apply in different situations.

The most important point that may be made about the application of probability figures is that the untrained user of such figures is prone to make final statements or draw final conclusions, either favorable or adverse, about what is going to happen to a particular child or a particular group of children. Even when such final conclusions are not intended by the examiner or other persons working with the figures, the lay person concerned deeply with the meaning of the data, perhaps a parent or a professional worker, may, in all honesty, misunderstand unskilled interpretations of the test results and so come to unwarranted conclusions. This eventuality is unfortunately always a likely one, but it is more likely to occur when reports are made by inexperienced clinicians.

It is a pertinent challenge to be asked what training or experience is necessary for proper use of these instruments. No final answer can be given. The MMPI, for example, is restricted in its distribution by ethical rules which govern the producer. This control over distribution is exercised in the hope on the one hand that incompetent persons will be discouraged from using the device and on the other hand that competent persons will be protected and encouraged to increase their competency through the valuation placed upon it. But such control is not alone adequate assurance. In situations where the psychologists or other responsible clinicians are certified or licensed either nationally or locally in professional certification programs, such certification should be adequate assurance of competence. If a certified or licensed clinician goes beyond his training or capabilities, he is subject to the controls of his own profession. In other situations, the clinician should have had at least some specialized training in the interpretation of objective test data and supervised experience in the interpretation of particular personality devices that may be used by him in evaluation of groups or individuals.

One additional difficulty inherent in all questions regarding the competence of the person who is to apply such tests is that there are a number of levels of use. At the simplest level in using the MMPI, for example, the competence can include only that required for obtaining a proper test-taking attitude in the persons being tested and the clerical and other skills necessary to identify the code category into which the profiles are to be placed. At the next level, the probability tables could be used for an indication of the degree to which figures may apply to the categories in question. If no further interpretations were involved, the clinician would not need to be trained at the highest levels of competence. The difficulty here is that in the practical situation it is so tempting to go further and make more comprehensive statements. The whole situation reduces only in part to training and competency; it also includes the responsibility of the clinician to govern his actions according to the dictates of accepted clinical practice.

In conclusion we would again stress our conviction that these studies provide simple data of immediate practical value. The validities and reliabilities of these data are far from perfect and we are sure that these can in time be improved. But we are endeavoring to encourage the immediate application of the MMPI with its widely used and familiar scales to initiate a general approach to the study of delinquency. We believe this objective personality test approach to be, with all its limitations, much superior to the present practices in which evaluating need and effectiveness of treatment and preventive programs, if done at all, employs subjective methods that have not even been validated.

References and Index

References

1. Bard, P. A note on MMPI (Pd) scores of state training school boys. *Minn. Counselor,* 4:21 (1950).
2. Blair, W. R. N. A comparative study of disciplinary offenders and non-offenders in the Canadian Army, 1948. *Canad. J. Psychol.,* 4:49–62 (1950).
3. Boynton, P. L., and B. M. Walsworth. Emotionality test scores of delinquent and non-delinquent girls. *J. abn. soc. Psychol.,* 38:87–92 (1943).
4. Capwell, Dora F. Personality patterns of adolescent girls. I. Girls who show improvement in IQ. *J. appl. Psychol.,* 29:212–28 (1945).
5. Capwell, Dora F. Personality patterns of adolescent girls. II. Delinquents and non-delinquents. *J. appl. Psychol.,* 29:289–97 (1945).
6. Clark, J. H. Clinical use of the Altus thirty-six point adjustment test in screening army AWOL's. *J. consult. Psychol.,* 12:276–79 (1948).
7. Clark, J. H. Application of the MMPI in differentiating AWOL recidivists from non-recidivists. *J. Psychol.,* 26:229–34 (1948).
8. Clark, J. H. Additional applications of the Altus thirty-six point adjustment test as a screening instrument. *J. gen. Psychol.,* 40:261–65 (1949).
9. Clark, J. H. The adjustment of army AWOL's. *J. abn. soc. Psychol.,* 44:394–401 (1949).
10. Clark, J. H. The relationship between MMPI scores and psychiatric classification of Army general prisoners. *J. clin. Psychol.,* 8:86–89 (1952).
11. Cook, C. D. A comparison of the personal adjustment inventory scores of criminal and normal male subjects. Seminar thesis, Depauw University, 1948.
12. Doll, E. A., and K. A. Fitch. Social competence of juvenile delinquents. *J. crim. law & Criminol.,* 30:52–67 (1939).
13. Drake, L. E. A social I.E. scale for the MMPI. *J. appl. Psychol.,* 30:51–54 (1946).
14. Durea, M. A., and M. H. Fertman. Emotional maturity of delinquent girls. *Amer. J. Orthopsychiat.,* 11:335–38 (1941).
15. Ellis, A., and H. S. Conrad. The validity of personality inventories in military practice. *Psychol. Bull.,* 45:385–426 (1948).
16. Faris, R. E. L., and H. W. Dunham. *Mental Disorders in Urban Areas.* Chicago: University of Chicago Press, 1939.
17. Fisher, R. A., and F. Yates. *Statistical Tables for Biological and Medical Research.* London: Oliver and Boyd, 1948.
18. Freeman, F. N., and C. D. Flory. Growth in intellectual ability as measured by repeated tests. *Monogr. Soc. Res. Child Developm.,* 2, No. 2, 1937.
19. Freeman, R. A., and H. M. Mason. Construction of a key to determine recidivists from non-recidivists using the MMPI. *J. clin. Psychol.,* 8:207–8 (1952).
20. Fry, F. D. A study of the personality traits of college students and of state prison inmates as measured by the MMPI. *J. Psychol.,* 28:439–49 (1949).
21. Fry, F. D. A normative study of the reactions manifested by college students and

by state prison inmates in response to the Minnesota Multiphasic Personality Inventory, the Rosenzweig Picture-Frustration Study, and the Thematic Apperception Test. *J. Psychol.*, 34:27–30 (1952).

22. Gjerdi, C. M. Parent-child resemblances in vocational interests and personality traits. Unpublished Ph.D. thesis, University of Minnesota, 1949.

23. Glenn, R. A study of personality patterns of male defective delinquents as indicated by the MMPI. Unpublished M.S. thesis, Pennsylvania State College, 1949.

24. Glueck, S., and Eleanor Glueck. *Juvenile Delinquents Grown Up.* New York: The Commonwealth Fund, 1940.

25. Glueck, S., and Eleanor Glueck. *Criminal Careers in Retrospect.* New York: The Commonwealth Fund, 1943.

26. Glueck, S., and Eleanor Glueck. *Unraveling Juvenile Delinquency.* New York: Hildreth Press, Inc., 1950.

27. Goodenough, F., and J. E. Anderson. *Experimental Child Study.* New York: Century Company, 1931. Pp. 234–38, 501–12.

28. Gough, H. G. A sociological theory of psychopathy. *Amer. J. Sociol.*, 53:359–66 (1948).

29. Gough, H. G. A new dimension of status: I. Development of a personality scale. *Amer. Soc. Rev.*, 13:401–9 (1948).

30. Gough, H. G. A new dimension of status: II. Relationship of the St scale to other variables. *Amer. Soc. Rev.*, 13:534–37 (1948).

31. Gough, H. G. Factors relating to the academic achievement of high school students. *J. educ. Psychol.*, 40:65–78 (1949).

32. Gough, H. G., and others. A scale for measuring social responsibility. In press.

33. Gough, H. G., and others. A scale for measuring dominance. In press.

34. Hathaway, S. R. The personality inventory as an aid in the diagnosis of psychopathic inferiors. *J. consult. Psychol.*, 3:112–17 (1939).

35. Hathaway, S. R. A coding system for MMPI profile classification. *J. consult. Psychol.*, 11:334–37 (1947).

36. Hathaway, S. R., and J. C. McKinley. *Manual for the MMPI* (revised). New York: The Psychological Corporation, 1951.

37. Hathaway, S. R., and P. E. Meehl. *An Atlas for the Clinical Use of the MMPI.* Minneapolis: University of Minnesota Press, 1951.

38. Kelley, T. L., G. M. Ruch, and L. M. Terman. *Stanford Achievement Tests: Manual of Directions.* Yonkers-on-Hudson, New York: World Book Company, 1940.

39. Kuhlmann, F. *Tests of Mental Development.* Minneapolis: Educational Test Bureau, 1939.

40. Lowrey, L. G. Delinquent and criminal personalities. In J. McV. Hunt (ed.) *Personality and the Behavior Disorders,* Vol. II, pp. 794–821. New York: Ronald Press, 1944.

41. Meehl, P. E., and S. R. Hathaway. The K factor as a suppressor variable in the Minnesota Multiphasic Personality Inventory. *J. appl. Psychol.*, 30:525–64 (1946).

42. Monachesi, E. D. Some personality characteristics of delinquents and non-delinquents. *J. crim. law & Criminol.*, 38:487–500 (1948).

43. Monachesi, E. D. Personality characteristics and socio-economic status of delinquents and non-delinquents. *J. crim. law & Criminol.*, 40:570–83 (1950).

44. Monachesi, E. D. Personality characteristics of institutionalized and non-institutionalized male delinquents. *J. crim. law & Criminol.*, 41:167–69 (1950).

45. Nikolaisen, Katherine. The Minnesota Occupational Scale. Mimeographed by the Institute of Child Welfare, University of Minnesota.

46. Perlman, M. Social class membership and test-taking attitude. Unpublished M.A. thesis, University of Chicago, 1950.

47. Pressey, S. L., and L. C. Pressey. Development of interest-attitude tests. *J. appl. Psychol.*, 17:1–16 (1933).

48. Schuldt, L. Histories and present programs of home schools for boys in Hennepin and Ramsey Counties (Minn.), 1941–1942. Unpublished M.A. thesis, University of Minnesota, 1942.
49. Shaw, C. R., and H. D. McKay. *Report on the Causes of Crime, Vol. II*. Washington, D.C.: National Commission on Law Observance and Enforcement, 1932.
50. Terman, L. M. *Mental and Physical Traits of a Thousand Gifted Children*. Stanford: Stanford University Press, 1926.
51. Terman, L. M., and C. C. Miles. *Sex and Personality*. New York: McGraw-Hill, 1936.
52. Terman, L. M., and Melita H. Oden. *The Gifted Child Grown Up*. Stanford: Stanford University Press, 1947.
53. Vanvorst, R. B. An evaluation of test performances of a group of psychopathic delinquents. *Psychol. Bull.*, 50:583 (1943).
54. Warner, W. L., M. Moeker, and K. Eels. *Social Class in America*. Chicago: Science Research Associates, 1949.
55. Washburne, J. N. A test of social adjustment. *J. appl. Psychol.*, 19:125–44 (1938).
56. Wechsler, D. *The Measurement of Adult Intelligence*. Baltimore: Williams and Wilkins Company, 1944.
57. Welsh, G. S. An extension of Hathaway's MMPI profile coding. *J. consult. Psychol.*, 12:343–44 (1948).
58. Welsh, G. S. Some practical uses of MMPI profile coding. *J. consult. Psychol.*, 15:82–84 (1951).
59. Wiener, D. N., and L. R. Harmon. Subtle and obvious keys for the MMPI: Their development. Advisement Bull., Minneapolis VA Regional Office, No. 16, 1946.

Index

Academy samples, in Monachesi study, 40, 41

Adolescents: general characteristics of, 7–8, 17, 18, 24–25, 43, 96, 98, 108; and use of MMPI, 16, 24–25, 87, 88

Adults: attitudes toward deviations, 7; MMPI scales derived from, 9, 22; contrast with characteristics of youth, 24–25, 43; norms of, 41; compared with ninth-graders, 102–5, 108; comparison of delinquents with adult clinical cases, 123, 136, 137

Age, as sampling factor: in Monachesi study, 39, 40, 41; in Ashbaugh study, 55; in Lauber-Dahlstrom study, 63; in Hathaway *et al.* study, 70; in Hathaway-Monachesi study, 87, 93, 109

Aggression, 68, 69, 108. *See also* MMPI scales: SCALES 4 and 9

Alsea high school, Ore., 54

Arsonists, 18

Ashbaugh, James H., 13, 54

Asocial behavior, 5, 8, 17, 18, 23, 24, 27, 52, 59, 134, 136. *See also* Psychopathic deviate; MMPI scales: SCALE 4

Atlas for the Clinical Use of the MMPI, 14, 20, 22, 73, 125: study program in, 25–28

Bellevue Adult Intelligence Scale, 63

Benton County, Ore., 54, 55

Boynton, P. L., 36

Broken homes, as delinquency factor, 3, 5, 50, 51, 53

Cannot Say score, *see* MMPI scales: ? SCALE

Capwell, Dora F., 5, 12, 13, 29, 38, 49, 51, 52, 65, 70, 71, 80, 107

Case records, 91: limitations for personality analysis, 4

Chi square, applied in Hathaway *et al.* study, 73, 78, 82

Clinical approach: to delinquency, 8–9; of MMPI, 13, 14, 48; needed for interpretation of profiles, 23, 138–39

Clinical scales, 13, 14, 16, 19, 20, 21, 41, 48, 56, 57, 58, 64, 65, 72, 90, 133, 134. *See also* MMPI scales: SCALES 0, 1, 2, 3, 4, 5, 6, 7, 8, 9

Coding, description of, 20–22. *See also* MMPI code patterns

College students, compared with ninth-graders, 101–2, 108

Compulsions, 18, 26, 43, 50, 108. *See also* MMPI scales: SCALE 7

Control groups: limitations of, 4; in Capwell study, 51, 52; in Ashbaugh study, 54, 55; in Hathaway-Monachesi study, 119, 121

"Conversion V," 23, 26

Cook, C. D., 59

Corvallis high school, Ore., 54

Cottle, William C., 25

Court procedures, with juveniles, 8–9, 137–38: variations in, 44, 49; in rural areas, 49, 53; in Oregon, 59; in Rock Island, Ill., 61–62, 64

D, *see* MMPI scales: SCALE 2

Dahlstrom, W. Grant, 13, 61

Dash, use in codes, 21. *See also* MMPI code patterns: – CODES

Defensiveness, 15, 16, 19, 38, 44, 45, 47, 51, 60, 123. *See also* MMPI scales: L SCORE, F SCORE, K SCORE

Delinquency, definitions of, 6–7, 29, 54, 59, 110

Delinquency probability numbers, *see* Probability numbers

"Delinquency scale," disadvantages of, 10–11

Depression, 16–17, 23, 26, 34, 35, 45, 96, 123. *See also* MMPI scales: SCALE 2